Ornamental Fish

Our Little Friends

Ornamental Fish
Our Little Friends

HONOS VERLAG

© Honos Verlag GmbH, a subsidiary of
VEMAG Verlags- und Medien Aktiengesellschaft, Cologne
www.apollo-intermedia.de

Authors: Willi and Ursula Dolder
Complete production: Honos Verlag GmbH, Cologne
Printed in Poland

Contents

Sarah Dickens.

Introduction

The Colourful World of Aquarium Fish

Next to birds, aquarium fish are the most popular pets in the world. Several million freshwater and saltwater fishes are kept in Great Britain, in aquariums ranging from the simple fish bowl to the elaborately equipped koi pond. Aquariums can be found not only in private households, but also in many doctors' practises, restaurants, conference rooms, hospitals and the reception halls of public buildings and banks—anywhere their beautiful colours and shapes can serve to entertain and enthral visitors.

In the past 50 years, the community of fish enthusiasts has grown explosively, increasing ten- or perhaps even hundred-fold, giving rise to a special industry that has taken on considerable economic impact, with sales in the billions year after year. Whenever pets become an interesting commercial prospect, however, there is always a risk that their needs will not be adequately taken into consideration. Looking at the example of aquarium fish, a disregard for the needs of living creatures can be discerned when inexpert beginners are not given the necessary comprehensive advice they need in purchasing and setting up their aquarium, or when a dealer or private breeder persuades the novice to buy fish that are difficult to keep and thus not appropriate for her or his level of experience.

This book about our silent, colourful friends seeks to help the interested beginner to explore a hobby that, with the right tools and knowledge at hand, is extraordinarily versatile and endlessly fascinating. The huge variety of aquariums, equipment, water plants, feed and of course fish species available today is quite overwhelming at first. Of the more than 12,000 existing species of freshwater fish, several thousand have found their way into our aquariums during the past few decades, together with a few hundred species of saltwater fishes, which are considerably more difficult to keep.

But there is no need for the beginner to feel daunted by this bewildering plethora of choices. After all, just 50 to 60 species account for over 90 % of all the ornamental fish kept in aquariums! In this book, we will concentrate on providing you with information on these popular varieties, rather than on a few exotic breeds that only rarely reach our shores.

Like a Fish in Water

cate when removed from their natural element. Although they require oxygen to live, just like mammals and birds, they are not equipped with lungs and therefore take in oxygen directly from the water via their gills. The few breeds that possess both lungs and gills include the Australian, African and South American lungfish. They are able to survive the dry season, when bodies of water in their habitat dry up, by burying themselves in mud.

Mudskippers, on the other hand, another kind of fish able to survive out of water, take an "emergency ration" of water with them for each foray onto land, breathing through their gills and sometimes through the mucous membranes of their mouth. In the course of several hundred million years of development, fish have conquered and settled almost every body of water on our planet: from crystal-clear mountain streams in the Alps, through the brackish water of tropical seas, to the strongly alkaline lakes in the East African Rift Valley; from the shallow, murky ponds of inland Australia to ocean depths thousands of meters below the surface!

African jewelfish

Nearly all of the 35,000 species of fish that inhabit our planet's fresh or salt water can only survive underwater. Since they are unable to breathe air, they soon suffo-

Congo tetra

The Natural Habitat of Ornamental Fish

Almost all of the fish breeds that we keep in conventional fresh- or saltwater aquariums come from the tropics, and less frequently from sub-tropical zones. The 50 or 60 aquarium species mentioned above are nowadays bred almost exclusively in captivity and no longer come directly from tropical waters. Ornamental fish-breeding grounds yielding an especially abundant variety of species can be found in South America, in sub-Saharan Africa and in South and Southeast Asia. In these areas they have taken over mainly the shallow zones near the shores of lakes and slow-flowing streams and rivers, along with certain niche habitats, i.e. areas that are not already dominated by other, stronger species. Many of these breeds' names indicate where they originated: Sumatra barb, Congo tetra, Siamese fighting fish and Ceylonese combtail, just to name a few.

Fish biotope in northern Australia

11

Ceylonese combtail

Opposite: Male swordtails

In general, these primarily small fish inhabit biotopes that offer them plenty of hiding places in the form of water plants, rotting branches and tree trunks, and stone caverns. In Lake Malawi and Lake Tanganyika in East Africa, however, several hundred species of cichlids have developed that live mainly in the plant-free, clear water near the shore.

Given the wide variety of completely different habitats in which our aquarium fishes live, it is extremely important to know where and in what environment the various breeds are found and feel at home. The same is true for determining the right water temperature and deciding which fish can share an aquarium. Some varieties spend almost all their time close to the ground or in the lowest regions of the biotope and others like to swim close to the surface, while yet other fish prefer the middle zones.

Another factor of vital importance is the chemical composition of the water, i.e. the pH values, the hardness of the water, its nitrate and nitrite content and the concentration of various gases, just to mention a few of the key elements to consider. But have no fear: you definitely don't have to be a chemistry whiz in order to be able to create and maintain a watery environment that will make the most common varieties of aquarium fish feel right at home.

In the following chapters we will take a step-by-step approach to helping you put together the "ideal aquarium" that will offer the fish you select a home that meets all their needs. Your aquarium is sure to provide you with an exciting hobby that doesn't require a high investment of time or money, but will nonetheless fascinate you and your family for years to come.

The Right Home
for Your Fish

A public aquarium

Put very simply, aquariums are water-filled containers for all kinds of fish and plants. These are available today in a bewildering variety of shapes and sizes. Even after consulting shop personnel, buyers are often at a loss as to which aquarium is just right for their needs. We would therefore advise you to ask yourself some important questions before making a purchase, and perhaps ask your friends to help you find the answers. This means, first of all, to try to abstain from an impulse purchase—perhaps after returning from a fish exchange or a public aquarium.

Aquariums are small ecosystems and, correctly put together, bring a beautiful and fascinating aspect of nature into your home. In the chapter on Biotope Aquariums, the master of aquarium photography and book author Klaus Paysan provides knowledgeable advice on setting up and successfully maintaining these kinds of tanks, sharing his wealth of experience on the topic. But even if you merely want to keep a few colourful fish in some water and do not have exacting demands as to aquarium plants and furnishings, there are a few important things to keep in mind. For example, you should be aware that even the tiniest, 25-millimetre guppy needs an aquarium that suits its needs, with various hiding places, the right composition of substances in the water and an appropriate water temperature. Goldfish bowls or glass jars are by no means proper containers for highly developed living creatures—whether goldfish or other species.

Frame, Panorama or All-glass Aquarium?

The aquarium you choose depends of course on its intended use, but also on how much you are willing or able to spend. If you would like the aquarium to be a decorative highlight in your home, you might be inclined to make a large investment in a 300- or 400-litre tank and ask a professional to set it up for you. But if you view ornamental fish more as an active hobby, you will have different ideas on what you need in an aquarium. The size is perhaps more important than the form, and the location depends on the needs of the fish and not the suggestions of your interior decorator. There are three basic types available: the frame or picture frame aquarium, the full-glass tank and the all-glass tank.

All-glass Aquariums Are a Good Buy

The latter variety is the most common, and it is also the least expensive. It is made of glass panels—in the more expensive ones polished plate glass, and in the cheaper ones window glass—which are glued together using a non-toxic silicone rubber of the kind that can be purchased in aquarium shops. It doesn't take any special skills to make this kind of aquarium yourself. All you have to do is ask a glazier to cut you glass plates in the desired sizes, having him bevel the edges so you don't hurt yourself when working with them. The thickness of the glass plates depends on the size of the finished aquarium. For a tank sized 60 x 40 x 40 cm (which will hold about 100 litres), the glass should be 5 mm thick on the sides, and 7–8 mm thick on the bottom. If the aquarium is to be 100 x 50 x 60 cm (length x width x height), it will hold something like 300 litres of water and the glass must therefore be correspondingly thicker: 10 mm at the sides and 12 mm on the bottom. If the required thicknesses are not available, opt for somewhat thicker, rather than somewhat thinner, glass. Then you can purchase special silicone rubber glue at the aquarium store, which

Various swordtails

comes in cartridges of various sizes. Well-stocked dealers can offer you a sheet of instructions on how to use the silicone glue. If not, perhaps you're better off taking your business to a different store! After degreasing (e.g. with acetone), cleaning and drying the glass, lay it on an even surface, for example a table, and glue the pieces together. In the beginning, until you've had some practice, your rubber seal might be a bit uneven. You can neaten it up with your finger, after moistening it with soapy water or washing up liquid to prevent the rubber from sticking.

Silicone rubber takes 48 hours or longer to dry, depending on the humidity in the air. Larger tanks, from about 100 litres up, should be stabilised along the top longitudinal axis with glass strips about 5 cm wide and 12 mm thick. These glass strips can also serve later as a place to rest a cover and/or lamps you might want to add to your tank.

Of course it's easier just to purchase a ready-made aquarium, and perhaps even let an expert set it up for you. There are tanks as small as 10 litres

Tip
Some aquarium clubs, and even larger shops, offer aquarium building courses from time to time. This allows you to put your own aquarium together in the course of two or three evenings with the helpful support of experts.

Information

The frame aquarium is made, as the name suggests, of a metal or plastic frame into which glass plates have been glued. In a panorama aquarium only the base and upper frame are made of metal or plastic, while the side panels are not held by a frame but are glued together directly with silicone rubber.

Community tank in living room (frame aquarium)

available, but these are at the most suitable for use as breeding tanks or quarantine stations for sick or newly purchased fish. Your aquarium should be a minimum of 60–70 litres in size, and a bit bigger is even better for ensuring an ecological balance between plants and fish, water and pH. The costs for the necessary technical equipment are not much higher for a 100-litre tank than for one half that size.

All-glass and Frame Aquariums

Before high-strength silicone glue came onto the market, the only aquariums available were held together by a metal frame using, for example, ship's putty as glue, which after a time would become hard and brittle and begin to leak. Then the dripping aquarium would have to be mended, causing commotion and stress for fish and human alike. Today, the glass in all aquariums is glued with sili-

cone, which has a very long useful life and requires no maintenance.

Frame and panorama aquariums are quite a bit more expensive than all-glass tanks, and are therefore not readily available in smaller sizes. They are usually purchased only in 400–1,000-litre sizes as decorative features in public buildings and restaurants, but of course it is also possible to enjoy them in a private home. Just keep in mind that this amount of water is extremely heavy! You can calculate the amount of water a tank will hold by multiplying length times width times height and then dividing by 1,000. This sounds more complicated than it is.

For example: an aquarium measuring 100 x 50 x 50 cm can hold exactly 250 litres of water (when filled to the brim), in accordance with the formula 100 x 50 x 50 = 250,000 : 1,000 = 250 litres. A litre weighs about one kilogram, so 250 litres weigh 250 kilograms. Then you need to add the weight of the aquarium itself, plus the technical acces-

sories and the table or piece of furniture on which it's standing. A total weight of 350 kg is thus a realistic estimate of this not particularly large aquarium. Those who live in older apartments, particularly, should take this into account and make sure before they purchase an aquarium that the old wooden floorboards are able to bear the weight.

Naturally, it's not only possible to build an all-glass aquarium, but also the other two kinds, the panorama and frame aquarium. You will need the corresponding plastic, aluminium or iron frame or framework. These can be purchased in specialty shops. The latter can be made to measure by a building fitter or metal worker. For these kinds of structures it is important to make sure that all surfaces that come into contact with the glass are completely even. Otherwise, the high water pressure will sooner or later cause the glass to crack or even the whole aquarium to burst!

As in all-glass aquariums, glass plates of the correct thickness are glued together using silicone rubber. You can usually expect a drying time of 24 hours per 0.5 cm rubber thickness.

Clown rasbora

Location is Key

Not too long ago, some aquarium owners were of the opinion that fish should get at least a few hours of sunlight each day. They placed the tank near a window where it would be exposed to direct sunlight in the morning or evening, or even put it on the windowsill (as is still the case in many classrooms today!) The consequences

Firemouth cichlid

included an overgrowth of algae, and water temperatures too high for even warmwater fish or plants. Often, fish were mysteriously found dead for no apparent reason.

With today's lighting technology, the tank can be placed practically anywhere in the room, although, as mentioned above, the weight of the tank should be taken into consideration. Heavy aquariums weighing far more than 100 kg should be placed near a wall and only used as room dividers if the owner is absolutely certain of the weight-bearing capacity of the floor. If you live on the ground floor with no cellar below, weight is of course not an issue for you. The same goes for aquariums set up in the cellar.

Good places for an aquarium are the corner or wall opposite a window in the living room or office. The tank is then far enough away from daylight that algae will not be stimulated to proliferate and the sun will not be reflected in the glass. In addition, it is important to remember that most tropical fish varieties live in water that is murky or strongly coloured (by suspended particles), or in water flowing through forested areas with very little sunlight filtering through to the ground or river—meaning that lighting conditions are usually dim at best.

If your house is frequently subjected to vibrations caused by trains, trams or trucks driving by, you need to be especially careful in choosing the location for your aquarium. Otherwise, this movement could cause the glass to crack or might disturb the fish and disrupt their natural behaviour. These vibrations can be cushioned to a certain extent by not placing the aquarium on the bare floor, but rather on a thick felt pad or PVC panel.

Once a location has been found that all family members agree on, and the bearing capacity of the floor has been confirmed, you need to decide whether to place the aquarium on a wood or metal base or on top of a piece of furniture. Here, too, the weight of the tank is a decisive factor. For heavier aquariums, a base made of square pipe 3–4 cm in width, welded together in the size of the aquarium and 50–70 cm high, is a better choice than a wooden framework. You can paint the metal base to go with the rest of the furnishings and add curtains or doors behind which you can store all of the technical equipment and utensils you'll need for the aquarium: pumps, heating units, outside filters, fish food, scoop nets, extra rocks, roots and so forth. The weight of the aquarium should be distributed over as large a surface as possible. That means not only over the frame itself, but also over a 25–30 mm thick plywood board placed on top of the frame. The larger the tank, the more important it is that it rest absolutely evenly on its base, to ensure that no tensions are created in the glass plates that might cause them to crack. A 5–10 mm thick styrofoam panel is the ideal cushion between aquarium and furniture or base.

Information

Aquariums are not really suitable for the bedroom, since the pump, filter and aeration do not work in complete silence—even if modern devices only hum gently. The ideal place is somewhere people can sit down and enjoy the entertainment provided by the fish, which is more original and has more variety than anything on TV!

Redhead cichlid in mating condition

If the aquarium is 80 kg or heavier, it's much better to set it up in place before adding gravel and water—otherwise you will just be making more work for yourself, because a filled aquarium is so heavy that it cannot and should not be carried around.

Cold or Warmwater Fish?

In the next chapters, we will provide you with step-by-step instructions on how to furnish your aquarium. But before you get started, let's look at the question of whether cold or warmwater fish are better for the beginner.

If you visit a fish store or look around at the aquariums owned by most long-term enthusiasts, you will notice that virtually all of the aquariums you encounter are home to brightly coloured, often iridescent fish with elaborate markings or fins. The expert will recognise immediately that such fish almost always come from tropical waters in South America, Africa and Asia, and only rarely from more temperate regions. These tropical and sub-tropical guests are used to temperatures in their home habitats that are much warmer than those found in Europe and which are hardly subject at all to daily or seasonal fluctuations. Temperatures might usually go down by 1 °C or 2 °C at night and be somewhat colder during the monsoon season than during the dry period. Nevertheless, these fluctuations are minimal.

Our local waters, by contrast, undergo enormous temperature changes. Our indigenous fish species have adapted to these fluctuations, but no stranger from warmer climes could survive them. The European and North American fish species can't really compare to their exotic cousins in colourfulness and attractiveness. They usually display subdued colours—with the notable exception of the three-spined male stickleback during brooding—and even when swimming

Red shiner

together as a school do not offer the obvious appeal of neon, Congo or glowlight tetras. Only some breeds of goldfish and the kois from Japan, a species of carp, can hold their own with the warmwater varieties.

Hence, the decision for or against cold or warmwater fish can be reduced to a—somewhat simplified—equation: do I want small, active and colourful fish that bring life to my living room aquarium? Or would I prefer fish that are not much to look at, but which are less demanding in terms of water quality, oxygen content and food than the warmwater species? Most beginners understandably choose the warmwater fish. Thanks to the support provided by most of the pet shops and fish stores, keeping the most widespread and popular breeds has become quite easy, hardly posing a problem even for the novice.

If you still decide to try your hand at keeping coldwater fish, in the second half of the book (p. 118 ff.) you'll find some tips on their care and a summary of the species that are best suited to an unheated tank or a garden pond in the summer.

Technical Requirements

Information

Without human intervention, streams and rivers, as well as ponds and lakes, are regularly or sporadically supplied with fresh water, whose functions include bringing in new oxygen and washing away debris. In our comparatively tiny aquarium these natural processes can work only with the help of various tools.

Heater, filter and other equipment

As already mentioned above, almost all of our colourful fish friends come from tropical waters in which temperatures stay between approximately 22 °C and 28 °C the whole year round.

We therefore can't simply place them in room-temperature water, but must use a heater to achieve a constant warm temperature. Aquariums are like natural habitats in miniature and usually contain water, gravel, plants and fish. Unlike the large bodies of water where the fish come from, however, in the aquarium they are no longer part of a balanced ecosystem but rather live in an artificially created world.

We need to make sure the water stays clean by channelling it through a filter that removes debris and toxins. Usually the aquarium also needs to be aerated using an air pump that supplies fresh oxygen and also creates the currents in the water that make many species feel at home.

In addition to heater and filter, the minimum standard technical equipment for an aquarium also includes artificial lighting. This ensures that plants and fish receive just enough light, but not too much, and also provides for the best visual presentation of the tank. Let's take a brief look at each of these technical elements in turn.

The Heater

The source of heat used most often by aquarium beginners, adequate for tank sizes up to about 500 litres, is the tube heater. The heating element, encased in a glass tube, is warmed up electrically and radiates this warmth into the water. Heaters are available in many sizes and wattages. They are fastened with suction cups to the side of the aquarium, at best in a rear corner. The tubes are usually dyed green to camouflage them but are still not particularly attractive. They can be placed unobtrusively so not as to disturb the aesthetics of the aquarium—perhaps behind a large plant or root—but always where the water can circulate around them. If there is not enough water circulation, the corner where the heater is will be warm and

the rest of the tank will be considerably cooler.

The temperature of the water must be monitored regularly with a thermometer placed as far away from the heating element as possible. If you use a conventional glass thermometer, this should be fastened inside the aquarium in such a way that you can easily read it. Liquid crystal thermometers, however, are attached outside the glass. They indicate the water temperature with a colour scale and are very dependable, inexpensive and unbreakable. The most expensive variant is a system in which a probe is hung or laid in the water and the temperature is then displayed digitally on a small box mounted outside the tank.

A substantially more expensive but also more versatile alternative is to heat the aquarium with a thermofilter. This useful device, which is mounted outside the tank, has a filtering function—which we will come to later on—and also heats the filtered water to the desired temperature before directing it back into the tank. In the process of doing so, it fulfils a third function by circulating the water and adding oxygen.

A thermofilter offers certain advantages over tube heaters and conventional filters. First, the heating performance is coordinated with that of the filter, and the installation efforts required are minimal: all that's necessary is a feed pipe for the filtered and warmed water and a temperature sensor that reports the values back to the control unit. A tube heater or thermofilter must be the appropriate size for the aquarium. A 100-litre tank has no need for a 500-watt heating unit. As a rule of thumb, a tank which is located in a heated living room or office will require about 0.5 watts of heating performance for every litre of water. For the 100-litre tank described, a tube heater with an output of 50–60 watts is sufficient.

The desired water temperature can be set using the thermostat in the tube heater or with a separate temperature control unit. Two, three or even more heaters in various aquariums can be hooked up to this control unit. If you opt for a thermofilter, however, you need only follow the manufacturer's instructions, as long as you choose the correct size for your tank. Small thermofilters are suitable for aquariums sized up to about 300 litres, while larger ones can be used for 600 or more litres. They are capable of circulating 500–750 litres of water per hour, guiding it through the filter and keeping it consistently at the required temperature.

Black mollies

25

The Filter

Every bit as important as the heater is the aquarium filter. The filter's job is to keep the water clean and clear, maintaining the fragile ecological balance. Food scraps spoil very rapidly in warm water, fish excrement reduces water quality, and rotting plant parts must be removed.

With an interior filter, the filter and filter material are found within the aquarium and with an exterior filter, outside of the tank—for example hidden in the base. But both types of filter work according to the same principle: water is sucked in by a pump behind the filter and conducted through the filter substrate. This might be made of fine-pored foam, a special kind of porous glass, filter charcoal, ceramic, lava granulate or gravel. It retains debris mechanically or uses biological or chemical means to transform toxic compounds into non-toxic ones.

It is in the nature of things that filters fill up relatively quickly with pollutants. This then hampers their functioning. The filter medium must therefore be cleaned or replaced from time to time, depending on its capacity. If the filter material in use is light-coloured foam or special glass, you can tell by its discolouration and darkening when it's time to clean it. The filter substrate is rinsed several times in warm water—without any cleaning agents—until the water runs off clear. Then it can be used again. In an aquarium with a normal population, the filter medium will need to be cleaned every two to four weeks and replaced with new material about twice a year.

Interior or Exterior Filter?

Interior filters are used wherever they do not diminish the aesthetics of the aquarium, such as in larger landscape or community aquariums. But they can also be used in smaller tanks under 100 litres. The smallest filters are suitable for tanks of 20 or 40 litres. The filter volume for these is less than 90 cm^3, and the pump moves some 50–150 litres of water per hour. Their outer dimensions are modest: 130 x 60 x 50 mm. At the opposite end of the scale, devices designed for aquariums of 200 litres and over have a filter mass of 600–700 cm^3, clean around 1,000 litres of water per hour and measure about 350 x 70 x 80 mm. Newer models can be filled with various filter media, which work either mechanically, chemically or biologically. They clean the water, set it in motion, and, through a small plastic tube and diffuser, supply it with fresh oxygen.

Exterior filters are less conspicuous. Probably their main advantage over the interior filters is easier access for cleaning. The filter media can be removed, cleaned or replaced without reaching into the tank (and possibly disturbing the fish). The dimensions of the exterior filters are somewhat greater than those of the interior type, but this is inconsequential since there is plenty of room to stow them outside the tank.

There are now exterior filters available even for small tanks containing 50–80 litres of water. They are hung on the outer back wall of the aquarium and have an impressive capacity of 200–300 litres per hour!

Incidentally, the newest filter generation from a variety of manufacturers uses amazingly little electricity; for most tank sizes (80–200 litres) just 5–15 watts are required.

To make the decision between interior or exterior filter as well as the choice of filter material easier for the novice, here are some guidelines:

- For tanks sized up to 100 litres, use a modern interior filter. However, use an exterior filter only for larger aquariums and only if you can stow it in such a way that it can't normally be seen.

Brown discus

Information

As with heaters, there are various filter systems available. The most common are interior or exterior filters. There are also variants such as ground and high-speed filters, and entire filter combinations for large tanks, which not only clean the water by mechanical and biological means, but also purify it. They monitor the salt content of the water, add carbon dioxide, transform toxic nitrate into hydrogen gas and provide a lively current in the aquarium.

- Be sure you are able to remove and replace the filter material with minimal effort (e.g. filter cartridges), so that the fish are disrupted as little as possible.
- Don't choose the least expensive product, but rather the most versatile one (allowing for various filter materials, connection options for oxygen supply, etc.)
- Start out using mechanical filters, i.e. foam, fibreglass or ceramic pipes, and then wait till you've gathered some experience before experimenting with chemical or biological filters. In the beginning, clean the filter material at shorter intervals—especially if, after furnishing the aquarium, you find there is a lot of water-born matter to be filtered out.

- Invest in a mechanical or an electric gravel vacuum cleaner for removing dead plant material, large food scraps and dead fish before these can clog the filter.

Scoop Nets, Algae Scrapers, Siphons and Other Utensils

At the aquarium store the hobbyist will find a huge selection of tools, most of which are either unnecessary or can be made at home with little effort. But there are a few utensils you should have on hand from the very start. One of the most important items you can hardly do without is a scoop net or glass fish catcher. Occasionally you will need to remove a fish from the tank—either

Tip: *If you are working with your aquarium and coming into contact with the water, always turn off any electrical equipment before you begin. Just one defective device—especially in connection with water—can be life-threatening. Especially recommended for safeguarding against electrical shocks is the use of a residual current circuit breaker, which can be purchased at any electrical shop or DIY store. It is plugged in between the mains outlet and the aquarium devices and interrupts the current within fractions of a second as soon as it is routed incorrectly, e.g. through a body.*

Motorised interior filter

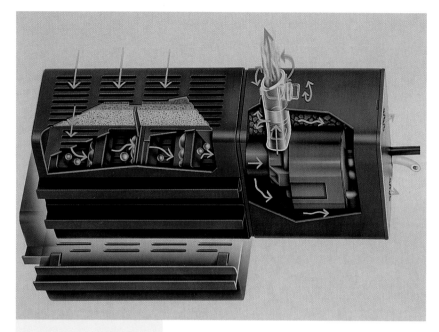

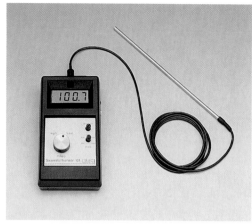

Motorised interior filter (above left) and device for measuring oxygen content (above right)

Scoop net

Algae scraper

because it seems sick, or because the tank is overpopulated, or because certain fish are fighting. The opening at the top of the scoop should be about the same size as your open hand. If it's any smaller, it will be hard to catch the fish. But if it's larger, it will be too hard to move the tool through the tank and between plants, stones and roots. Plant tongs are useful for removing dead leaves or sticking new plants into the gravel without putting your whole arm into the aquarium. These are available in various lengths and shapes. The best are 40–60 cm long and made of plastic so that there's no chance of oxidization or rust. With a little practice, you'll soon be able to pick up small items from the bottom of the tank—stones, root pieces, snails—and remove leaves or stem parts from plants.

Even with the best possible filter available, dead and rotting plant parts will eventually accumulate in the aquarium. They sink to the bottom and, if you wait too long to remove them, form a thick carpet which is anything but beneficial for the water quality. The easiest way to remove this mulm is with a gravel vacuum or mulm siphon that works either manually or electrically, with low voltage thanks to the built-in transformer.

Anyone who has ever had an aquarium can tell you that unbridled algae growth is always an annoyance. Even if no other water plants thrive, algae will proliferate and cling to everything, especially the glass. Strong algae growth indicates a disturbance in the ecological balance of the aquarium. The algae might be responding to too much light, too much plant fertilizer, too much food, too little filtering, or other factors. The simplest remedy, which however addresses only the symptoms, is the mechanical removal of the algae. If algae is clinging even to the plants and the furnishings, practically the only solution is to empty the aquarium and furnish it anew. But if the algae are primarily lining the glass, it can be removed with a glass scraper. This simple utensil usually consists of a scraper fitted with a replaceable razor blade. This is used to scrape off the algae horizontally and vertically. The algae can then be vacuumed out of the tank with the gravel vacuum. You should exercise extreme caution when scraping off the algae so as not to scratch the glass (either through fine quartz sand that gets into the blade or with the blade itself.)

Another helpful tool for fighting algae is a normal (but as yet unused!) scrubbing sponge. Instead of the aggressive green side, however, use the soft spongy side. For the stickier cases of algae, however, nothing but the scraper will do, or, as a very last resort, the "chemical club" (see p. 59).

Spare Parts to Have on Hand in Case of Emergency

In case the unexpected happens, namely a disruption in the normal functioning of your aquarium, it's always good to have a supply of spare parts at the ready. If you never have to use them—all the better. This includes a few metres of tubing with various diameters (10–20 mm), like the ones used for supplying filtered and heated water, or for the regularly required water exchange. Over time, exposure to heat and light can cause even soft plastic tubes to develop breaks and tears. This could (and often does) happen on a weekend or holiday when the shops are closed! But even without a filter (as long as it's not a thermofilter), the aquarium can be operated for a certain amount of time without difficulty.

If your fish are not getting enough oxygen, they will swim to the water's surface and gasp for air. To deal with a filter malfunction without having to purchase an expensive replacement unit right away, it's a good idea to have a small, inexpensive air pump on hand, as well as a few metres of plastic tubing that fits onto the pump valve. If the filter fails, then you can at least conduct some fresh air into the aquarium. If you connect the plastic tubing to a diffuser—usually a porous rock known as an airstone—then the air will rise from the bottom to the surface in small bubbles, gently circulating the water (for additional oxygen uptake) and enriching it with oxygen. This can keep the tank biologically intact for a few days.

Without a heater, however, it will soon be dead still in the aquarium. Fish that are used to temperatures of around

Sailfin molly

Fighting fish

25 °C do not long survive in water that is only 20 °C or under. It's therefore advisable to have a second heater on hand for emergencies. This reserve heater can be the simplest and least expensive kind of tube heater (perhaps an extra one owned by a friend who shares your hobby), as long as the water temperature can be held constant. Fluctuations of 2–3 °C are usually no problem for most types of fish.

The experienced aquarium owner often has the following items at his disposal: tube clamps, clips and connectors; silicone glue for small repairs; an extra glass cover for the aquarium (this is the part that cracks most frequently); replacement light bulbs; a thermometer; a small tank as a quarantine station; extra filter material; a so-called water test and maintenance kit (which can be used to check the chemical composition of the water at any time and, if necessary, to correct it—see p. 34 for details); and some emergency medications for the fish.

At least as important and as useful as the tools and spare parts described above, however, is a good relationship with an experienced aquarium owner or dealer who can even be reached on a Sunday.

Lighting—What Kind and How Many Hours?

Our ornamental fish primarily come from the tropics, where day and night are approximately equal in length—with 12 hours of light and 12 hours of darkness in each 24 hour period. The closer to the equator one goes, the smaller the fluctuation there is in the number of daylight hours. The further away from the equator, the greater the variance between summer and winter months. While we can enjoy up to 17 hours of daylight in the summer in our part of the world, in winter we have at most eight or nine. An aquarium that contains exotic fish— even those that have been bred in our climes for generations now—should be lit around 12 hours each day.

As discussed above, daylight is for various reasons not the appropriate light source. Our daylight is hardly comparable to the tropical sun in terms of colour spectrum, amount and intensity. A wide variety of aquarium lighting systems are available for purchase. The better, more expensive ones offer a colour spectrum that's ideal for plants and fish, while the less expensive systems can hardly be recommended and should only be used as an emergency stopgap. These are often sold as part of a complete package, i.e. an aquarium set consisting of tank, tube heater, interior filter and cover with light.

Sunlight changes its colour temperature as the day wears on. Early in the morning and late in the afternoon warm, reddish tones predominate, while during the day the blue spectrum comes to the fore. For aquariums, we need lamps with a high proportion of blue tones. The light bulbs usually used around the house are not appropriate for various reasons: they have too much red, provide too little light, and also develop considerable heat. Besides, the amount of electricity they use is much too high in relation to their performance. And although low-energy bulbs save on power, they still share the other negative characteristics associated with standard light bulbs.

The most frequently used lights for aquariums are fluorescent tubes, which come in various colour temperatures, including daylight, warm and white tones, as well as some with strong violet tones (these, however, tend to make plants and in particular red fish look unnatural). We recommend lighting using two different fluorescent tubes: one in daylight

and the other in a warm tone, for example a warm-toned and a white-toned tube.

For aquariums deeper than 60 cm, fluorescent tubes will hardly suffice. Water absorbs light strongly—especially if it is slightly brown due to the use of a peat filter or if it contains many suspended particles. Ten centimetres below

Black-spotted corydoras

An ideal lighting set-up

through thick vegetation. Unfortunately, they do generate a considerable amount of heat and therefore should not be mounted too close to the water's surface. If you choose this light arrangement, the aquarium obviously cannot be covered with a metal or plastic cover but only with a glass panel (covers also prevent fish from jumping out of the tank, for example if they are startled or chased by other fish).

Lighting—The Intensity is also Important

The strength of the lamps should be in proportion to the size of the aquarium, the clarity of the water and the light needs of the plants and fish. A rule of thumb is about 0.5 watts per litre of water. For a 100-litre tank this means about 50 watts of light are required (i.e. two tubes of 30 watts each) and for a 200-litre aquarium, 100 watts, i.e. three 30-watt tubes. The plants need more light than the fish!

Water with high nitrate concentrations also increases the light requirements of the vegetation. If they do not receive adequate light, the more sensitive plant varieties begin to wilt and rot.

Of course, not all varieties of fish and plants share the same light needs. In the chapter on aquatic plants (see page 46) we will introduce you to a few of the more robust species that a beginner can try out in her or his first aquarium. If the light is too bright for some of the fish, they can seek shade under the plants, or hide under roots and rocks. In their home habitats the light conditions are similar: there are sunlit patches of water, but also patches of shadow from trees and bushes.

A large amount of light, however, can lead to substantial algae growth; water snails and algae-eating fish species can offer some relief here. The rest is up to the aquarium owner equipped with scraper or sponge.

the surface, however, there is only 50 % as much light as above, and a mere 5 % of the light manages to penetrate through to 50 cm! Especially good for use as aquarium lights are the modern, albeit expensive, mercury vapour high-pressure lamps and the halogen metal vapour lamps. Both kinds are hung 10–20 cm above the aquarium, offer an abundance of light in daylight quality and are particularly good at penetrating

The aquarium light should remain on for 12 to 13 hours a day; this can be ensured most easily with an electric timer. You can program the timer to switch the light on and off automatically at the desired times. If the aquarium is not located in the bedroom but in a living room or office, it is usually convenient to switch the light on between five and six o'clock in the morning and switch it off again 12 to 13 hours later. The fish soon get accustomed to this rhythm, and in the evening, shortly before "lights out time", they will search out resting and sleeping places. With a dimmer you can even simulate a short dawn and dusk: the light gradually grows stronger over the course of ten minutes, for example, and in the morning the fish are not plunged into bright light from one second to the next, and plunged into darkness again at night. Expert opinions are divided as to the usefulness of such dimmers. Most agree that they exist more to give the aquarium owner a feeling of realistic morning and evening moods and don't actually benefit the fish or plants in any way.

Rosy barbs

South American aquarium

Information

It is not a good idea to turn off the aquarium light during the day and turn it on only in the early morning or evening hours, for example, or on dark winter days. Fish and plants need regular periods of light and dark that are anchored in their genetic material, and are sensitive to fluctuations.

Water—Elixir of Life

Note
Just as there are many different kinds of saltwater, fresh water varies widely as well. Its chemical composition depends on many factors, including the substances that enter the water from rain and run-off and those excreted into the water by plants and animals or which are generated through chemical reactions.

Swamp area in eastern Australia

Water—Elixir of Life

Nearly three-quarters of the earth's surface are covered with water, but only a small percentage is fresh water. The overwhelming majority is salt water with varying salt content.

The chemistry of water is quite well-known today and can be expressed using various values. The water hardness and the pH value are the two most important of these and the aquarium enthusiast should familiarise himself with their implications. In nature there is no such thing as "neutral", i.e. chemically pure, water. Water always contains a great deal of substances in solution (minerals, organic substances) and gasses. These have a decisive influence on the composition and the quality of the water. Water that is completely unpotable for us might be the ideal element for certain fishes and other living creatures, to which they have spent millions of years adapting. All of our ornamental fishes live in waters with very specific make-ups, which, depending on the location, might either be very stable or subject to continual fluctuations. In areas with marked dry periods and monsoon seasons, the water quality fluctuates widely over time, whereas the water composition in rainforest areas, for example, where it rains almost every day, is much more constant.

What Makes Water Hard or Soft?

Limescale in boilers or pots and pans is a sign of hard water, i.e. water that contains a large amount of dissolved magnesium and calcium salts. These in turn are present in great quantities in calciferous rock, where they are leached out by rainwater, for example, and washed into rivers and lakes. The less minerals water contains, the softer it is. It is well known that the soil of many tropical regions is exceptionally poor in minerals (which negatively effects its fertility). The water in these regions is therefore soft.

The total hardness of water (made up of the sum of all salts dissolved in it) can be determined using electronic measuring devices or, less precisely, but usually adequate for aquarium purposes, with indicator fluids, and expressed in °dH. The table below shows the °dH value for various types of water:

very soft water	from 0 to 4
soft water	from 5 to 8
medium-hard water	from 9 to 12
hard water	from 13 to 20
very hard water	over 20

Almost all ornamental fishes that come from South America, tropical Africa or

Southeast Asia live in natural habitats with soft to medium-hard water. Only a few groups, in particular the mouth-brooders from Lake Tanzania and Lake Malawi in East Africa, are used to medium-hard to hard water (these lakes are located in the middle of calciferous mountains).

Each fish has a range of tolerance in terms of the hardness of the water in which it can live, feel at home and breed. The smaller the tolerance, the more sensitive the species in question to fluctuations in water hardness that can occur due to chemical processes in any tank. Therefore, the beginner is best off starting out with fishes that are somewhat adaptable and that do not place high demands on water quality.

There is another hardness factor that also plays a role in the well-being of fish and plants: the carbonate hardness. In a tank with many plants and relatively few fish, which has an adequate oxygen supply, a medium carbonate hardness will come about all by itself. This is ideal for the water chemistry and we should "tamper" with it as little as possible. Only if you find that the pH values of the water are not stable should you approach an experienced aquarium owner or dealer for advice on how to handle this problem. These pH fluctuations might be connected with a carbonate hardness that is too high or too low. As long as you have less demanding and more tolerant fish varieties in your tank, the water chemistry does not play as crucial a role as with more sensitive breeds. Therefore, the beginner does not need to worry too much about aspects such as water hardness, carbonate hardness and pH values, and should be able to relax and enjoy her fish instead!

Freshwater angelfish

Some Remarks on Acidic and Alkaline Water

Next to the total hardness, the next most important factor for making sure water is appropriate for fish is the pH value. This value indicates if the water is neutral, acidic or basic (alkaline). We have no need to go into detail on the exact chemical formula or to explain

Three-way water test for measuring total water hardness, carbonate hardness and pH value

Longnose gar (Lepisosteus osseus)

the various degrees of acidity. Even for the experienced aquarium owner, some basic knowledge of chemistry will suffice.

The acid concentration of the water depends on positively and negatively charged ions and is partly the result of humic acids (organic substances) and carbon acid (anorganic). The pH scale begins at 1 (acid), with a middle value of 7 (neutral) and ends at 14 (alkaline). Therefore, all water under pH 7 is more or less acidic, and everything over that is alkaline or basic. Rainwater, with a value of about 7, is mostly neutral.

The majority of tropical ornamental fishes, especially those from rainforest areas such as the Amazon, Congo, Zaire and the river systems of Southeast Asia, live in waters with pH of about 5.5 to 7. Mouthbrooders from the huge, deep East African lakes do best at pH values around 8, i.e. alkaline, and some breeds from the flat, soda lakes of Kenya and Tanzania, for example Lake Nakuru, Lake Magadi and Lake Natron, even thrive in alkaline water with 10 to 11 pH. However, if one proceeds carefully, gradually adjusting the water over the course of days or weeks, they can also adapt to lower values.

Maintaining the proper pH value is a basic requirement for the well-being of the fish and in particular for successful breeding.

How can total hardness, carbonate hardness and pH value be adjusted?

Water values must be adjusted, for example, when you intend to breed fish and the particular species needs a certain total hardness and pH value for its young to develop properly. This also might be necessary if the water from your tap is especially hard, with high calcium carbonate content.

The total hardness in our climes will always be higher than that found where our tropical fishes originally come from. They usually live in soft water, with a low calcium carbonate concentration. Species that are not sensitive to water hardness will feel at home in our tap water and there will be no need to adjust it. The "South Americans" from the Amazon and other tropical rivers, on the other hand, need softer (softened) water.

Softer water, low in calcium carbonate, can be obtained in various ways. Smaller amounts, about 10 to 15 litres, can be made by boiling the water until the lime precipitates, or by simply buying distilled water and adding it to the aquarium water until the correct total hardness is then achieved. If you live in an area where peat is readily available, you can obtain soft water from a peat pit or pond and mix it in with the aquarium water.

If you have several tanks and have to soften the water regularly, it might be worthwhile purchasing what is called an ion exchanger, which removes salts from the water or, even better (and more expensive), a reverse osmosis system. This desalination technology is used with great success by oceangoing vessels as well as in the Arab States to desalinate saltwater in order to obtain fresh water. The water obtained through reverse osmosis is not only 98 to 99 % salt-free, it is also almost 100 % free of

Five-bar cichlid

bacteria, viruses and organic toxins and heavy metals.

In rare cases, for example when breeding East African cichlids or West African toothed carp, the water also has to be hardened, i.e. enriched with calcium carbonate. This is easy to do: you just add lime to the aquarium in the form of limestone or alabaster, or fertilise the plants with carbon dioxide. You can also purchase a total hardness generator (GH generator). The instructions will tell you exactly how much of the generator substance to add to the water.

For sensitive species of fish, or if you do not want to leave breeding up to chance, you will have to change the acidity (pH level) of the aquarium water to a value similar to that of the fishes' home waters. You can do so in the following ways:

Purchase a special peat-based liquid at the aquarium store and add it to the water according to the instructions. Or conduct the aquarium water through a peat filter, which gives it a light brown colour, but also the right pH value, somewhere between 6 and 7. If the pH value is to be raised above the neutral level of 7, as is necessary for some of the African cichlids and for saltwater fish, the easiest way to do this is with a powerful oxygen aeration. This drives most of the carbon dioxide out of the tank, causing the pH value to rise considerably. If aeration is not adequate, you can also add some sodium hydrogen carbonate (sodium bicarbonate) to the tank. 10 grams dissolved in water and added to a 100-litre tank change the pH value toward the alkaline direction. Our tap water is usually neutral or slightly

39

Dwarf cichlid pair

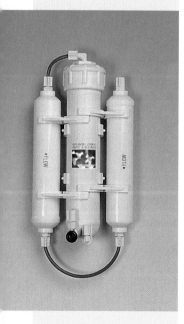

Reverse osmosis system

basic—the latter often brought about artificially in order to protect pipes from corrosion. All in all, you would only try to achieve an alkaline aquarium pH in rare cases.

Toxins in the Water

In waters with an intact ecological circulation there are no natural toxins that could possibly poison a river or a lake. But systems with this kind of ecological equilibrium are becoming increasingly rare. Even in remote areas, rivers and streams often manifest distressingly high levels of heavy metals, industrial salts, pesticides and fertilisers. The same goes for waters closer to home.

Everyone has heard about the alarming levels of toxins that can be found in the English Channel, rivers such as the Severn and the Trent, or lakes throughout agricultural areas and even in our drinking water—which comes in part

from exactly these sources! We thus have to assume that even the crystal-clear water that comes out of the tap is not as pure as it looks to the naked eye. Laboratory tests would prove that it contains, for example, chlorine, copper, iron, lead, cadmium, nitrates and other substances that are not good for ornamental fish. Even people living far out in the country can put a bucket under a gutter to catch virtually pH-neutral rainwater, but this water will still be anything but clean, pure and toxin-free!

In aquariums, however, the toxins in the water come primarily from the plants and fish themselves. In every living organism certain metabolic processes take place resulting in the excretion of waste products (urea and uric acid). In addition, aquarium plants die from time to time, in whole or in part, and food that is not consumed by the fish falls to the bottom of the tank and rots. Nitrogen concentrations rise to dangerous levels and can no longer be broken down completely by bacteria or held back by mechanical filters.

What can be done against toxins?

- First of all, it's good to keep in mind the old aquarium word of wisdom that a tank can hardly be underpopulated, but very easily overpopulated. How many fish can be kept in an aquarium is a topic we'll address later in the book.
- Second, the pH level should be checked now and again. In alkaline water—from about pH 7 and up—harmless ammonia can turn into aggressive ammoniac, a deadly poison for fish.
- Third, it's important to regularly remove plant and food remains. After a short time, if you exercise your observation skills you will have a good idea of how much your fish actually eat before the food falls to the bottom and is no longer consumed. With an electric gravel vacuum you can easily remove dead plants, mulm, food scraps and excrement that has collected at the lowest point in the tank.

Information

The aquarium owner must in general be satisfied with the water that comes out of his or her tap, or try to make it suitable for the aquarium using various means. There are a number of water conditioners on the market that can be added to the water to positively influence its chemical composition.

Fancy double swordtail guppies

41

• Fourth, don't forget to partially replace the water from time to time as recommended in the literature. In the early days of aquariums, people

Glass catfish

thought the animals would be happiest in stale, even amber-coloured old water. Today we know that this applies to very few species. Because in aquariums there is no natural supply of fresh water and draining out of older water, as exists even in the seemingly stillest and most current-free arms of the Amazon and the Congo, toxins and waste materials dissolved in the water can build up high concentrations. The nitrogen cycle goes off kilter or even breaks down altogether. Both plants and fish suffer and, sooner or later, losses are the inevitable consequence.

The best solution against toxins in the water is the above-described reverse osmosis system, which is available today even for smaller tanks—starting at about 100 litres. The osmosis is so effective that practically all toxins and salts are removed and microbe-free water is gen-

erated. But an easier and much less expensive way to keep the water clean is not to crowd the tank with fish, but rather to maintain a good ratio of plants and animals, not fertilising the former or feeding the latter in excess. With a little experience, you will find the "golden mean" and will not have to worry either about water values or the oxygen and carbon dioxide content of your aquarium.

Old Water out, New Water in

By contrast with earlier convictions that "old water" was especially good for ornamental fish, today it is recommended that the aquarium water be changed from time to time. As the days and weeks go by, toxins accumulate in the tank that can no longer be removed or neutralised by filters, medications or water conditioners. These dangerous substances include a rising salt content as well as highly poisionous ammoniac, which can develop when the pH value of the water is alkaline.

Every one to three weeks you should replace part of the aquarium water with fresh tap water. Warm water has a tendency to evaporate; the higher the water temperature in the tank and the lower the humidity in the room, the more water will be lost to the air. Cover plates prevent evaporation only in part, because no aquarium can or should be sealed airtight. In open aquariums that are lighted from above with haologen or high-pressure lamps, evaporation is of course especially rapid. 10 % or more of the water in the tank might be lost each week. Salts and toxins in the remaining water thus increase in concentration, meaning that it is necessary not only to top up the aquarium, but also to replace some of the old water. Before putting in new water, take the opportunity to vacuum the collected mulm and plant debris from the bottom of the tank.

The easiest way to change the water is to use a plastic tube with a diameter of about 15 to 20 mm as a siphon. Just place a 10 to 15-litre bucket on the floor next to the aquarium, put the tube in the tank, apply suction to get the flow started (either by sucking on the tube or

using a device especially designed for this purpose), and let the water drain into the bucket. In this way you can remove 20 to 30 % of the tank content and replace it with fresh water. It's better for the fish if the tap water you

Spotted tilapia
(Tilapia mariae)

Golden pencilfish
(Nannostomus beckfordi)

43

But don't worry: as long as you have beginner fish varieties, you do not need to concern yourself too much with the quality of the aquarium water. Temperature changes of up to 5 °C are likewise not a problem.

A partial water exchange should be undertaken at the latest when the water has taken on an amber hue. This comes from fish excrement and dead plants. If you use peat as filter material, the water will also be amber-coloured, but not necessarily "old". Another sign that water quality has deteriorated is odour. If the water smells stale or even foul, it's high time to add at least 50 % fresh water.

Ulrey's tetra
(Hemigrammus ulrey)

Opposite page:
Lambchop rasboras
(Rasbora heteromorpha)

Information

Changing all the water in the tank is a major procedure and in fact only needs to be done at the most once a year (and usually only every two years). The point at which this becomes necessary can be delayed by ensuring the proper balance of plants and fish in the tank—i.e. not over-populating the tank, but putting in a moderate amount of fish for its size. This makes for an easy-care aquarium and a beautiful addition to your home for years to come.

use has first been let stand for two to three days. If the water quality is poor—too much lime, heavy metals, nitrite and nitrate—you can improve it by using a water conditioner available in shops. As long as the fresh water in the bucket has reached room temperature, about 20 °C, it doesn't have to be warmed up to match the temperature of the aquarium water, unless you have a breeding tank with spawning and live-breeding fish. The water in a breeding tank is a few degrees warmer than in community tanks, and spawn and young fish are more sensitive to changes in temperature than adults.

Fresh water is also conducted into the tank using a tube. If, to save time, you try to pour it in directly from the bucket, the plants and fish will be subject to considerable turbulence, which is not good for either of them. In the case of sensitive fish like the discus, the water temperature as well as the pH values and water hardness must be tested after refilling the tank, and corrected if necessary. There are simple and accurate tests on the market today for measuring these three parameters, as well as for oxygen content, iron and copper concentrations, organic acids, ammoniac, phosphate, silicic acid and much more.

Completely Replacing the Water in the Tank

If you ever have reason to completely exchange all of the water in the tank—e.g. to refurnish the aquarium, if a fish disease has broken out, or if the ground cover has become completely soiled with fish and plant debris—this takes quite a bit more work than just exchanging 20 to 30 % of the water. To begin, all of the fish must be caught and placed in an extra tank. This is sometimes easier if you first drain off about a third of the water. If your work on the aquarium is only going to take a few hours, the fish can be left in a bucket—with a cover to prevent them from jumping out! But it's important to keep an eye on the temperature of the water in the bucket. It should not drop more than 4 to 5 °C below the accustomed temperature for any length of time. Otherwise, you will have to add warm water from time to time. If a substitute tank is available in which the fish can spend a few days, you can take your time in furnishing their permanent home and give the aquarium a thorough cleaning.

The water plants should be removed from the aquarium and placed in temperate water, and then all the furnishings can be taken out: rocks, roots, the ground material, the heater and filter.

The next step is to rinse the aquarium out with tap water in order to clean off any algae and dirt. Make sure not to scratch the glass with your cleaning implements. Small tanks can be cleaned carefully in the bathtub or a laundry room, while large ones must be cleansed in situ with the help of a suction tube. Once you've rinsed the tank a second time, add fresh gravel or thoroughly washed sand, lay out rocks and roots to form some new scenery, mount the technical apparatus (which you have first cleaned with a sponge or soft brush) and fill the tank halfway with fresh water.

Now you can replace the plants in new groupings. The ones that have developed well can be given pride of place, while the rotten or ailing ones can be replaced with some different varieties.

Once all the work on the aquarium is complete, fill the water up to a finger's width under the top and let stand for several days. Heater, filter, oxygen supply and lighting should already be in operation, soon creating the ideal conditions for the fish to be brought back from their temporary home to their community aquarium. The water is beautifully clear, colourless and transparent, the plants are putting down roots and the temperature is holding at the desired level.

If you have sensitive fish species and you're not absolutely sure of the water quality, you can first reintroduce some fish that are more tolerant of variations in pH and hardness. If they seem to be doing well, after one or two days you can put the rest of the fish into their redecorated, freshly filled aquarium. But, if while using a test system you discover that the new water quality greatly differs from the old, you will need to either add some water from the subsitute tank or use a water conditioner to improve quality.

The Right Plants

It takes a few weeks or even months before the vegetation in an aquarium starts to live up to its owner's expectations. The well-designed tanks in zoos and in the homes of experienced aquarium enthusiasts make it all look deceptively simple. But behind every lush aquarium habitat is a lot of hard work and a certain amount of knowledge and experience. Not only the fish have certain demands with regard to the quality of the water, its chemical composition, the lighting and food. As living organisms, our aquarium plants also need similar conditions to those found in their home habitats in order to thrive. These conditions include:

Water Hardness and pH Value

Both of these values should lie in the mid-range, i.e. a total hardness between 5 and 15 °dH, a carbonate hardness between about 5 and 10 °dH and a pH value between 6.5 and 7.3, that is between slightly acidic and slightly alkaline.

Lighting

Since they are used to different conditions in their natural habitat, not all plants require the same amount of light. The light should be on for at least twelve hours a day (near the equator day and night are of equal length). For tanks that are not unusually high (up to 50 cm), adequate light intensity can be calculated as 0.5 W per litre of water, supplied by daylight fluorescent tubes or metal vapour and high pressure lamps (see also p. 31 f.). It's best to put the lamps on a timer that automatically switches them on and off.

Clean Aquarium Cover, Clean Water

A soiled and scale-covered aquarium cover can swallow up a great deal of light, as can murky water. Swimming plants covering large sections of the water surface also prevent light from reaching the rest of the tank. The cover should be cleaned regularly, and 25 to 30 % of the water should be replaced every two to three weeks, not only for the benefit of the fish, but for the good of the plants as well (see p. 42 ff.). As you can see, both fish and plants require many of the same conditions.

Tank Bed and Fertilisation

The tank bed—which can range from tiny sand grains to coarse gravel—is a very important factor for helping plants thrive. Unlike in your garden, you can't simply add nutrient-rich humus to your aquarium substrate. However, aquatic plants have accustomed themselves to underwater conditions and are able to obtain the necessary nutrients from the excretions of the fish and food scraps, as well as getting the carbon dioxide (CO_2) they need for photosynthesis, which is "breathed out" by the fish, directly from the water. The CO_2 level can be kept constant using a special device, but this is only necessary for large tanks and sensitive plants. For smaller aquariums and less demanding plants, fertilisation now and then with a fertiliser in tablet form is fully sufficient. You can measure the CO_2 levels with a test kit available at the pet shop.

In addition to the nutrients mentioned above, which occur naturally in the aquarium, it also might be necessary to give your plants some supplemental fertiliser now and then. There are plenty of options available on the market, in particular liquid fertilisers, tablets or sticks. The plants take up these substances through their roots and leaves.

Please note, however: the liquid and stick fertilisers you might use for your garden and houseplants should under no circumstances be used to fertilise your aquatic plants!

Information

Plants not only enhance the looks of an aquarium; they often have very important tasks to fulfil. For one, they ensure that an equilibrium between flora and fauna can be achieved in the tank. For another, they offer the fish hiding places and a way to shield themselves from the light if necessary, as well as providing a spawning place and somewhere to raise their young. In addition, they provide the oxygen fish need to breathe and neutralise a whole series of toxins in the water. Naturally, the visual pleasure provided by a well-planted aquarium cannot be underestimated. Most aquarium owners view a tank in which plants and fish are thriving as a beautiful highlight in their home, which they care for with loving attention and proudly present to their guests.

To fertilise the plants in your aquarium, use products especially designed for this purpose and follow the manufacturer's instructions, especially with regard to the proper amount. Too much fertiliser places a burden on the water quality and chemistry and also leads to increased algae growth.

A furnished aquarium with swordtails and guppies

Broad-leaf ludwigia
(Ludwigia repens)

Rotala wallichii

A Plethora of Choices

To date some 4,000 plant species have been identified living in our planet's fresh water. Not even ten percent of these are offered in pet stores, but this still makes for quite an overwhelming selection for the aquarium owner.

When selecting plants, it's important not just to go by looks, i.e. the plants' attractiveness or dominance in the tank, but also to know exactly what you need and whether the plant is right for the aquarium you have in mind. There are plants that are only happy in soft water—these are commonly known as "lime-haters"—and others that are much more tolerant and will thrive in almost any water.

The same goes for water temperature. Some will do just as well at 20 °C as at 30 °C, while others, such as the beautiful but fussy Madagascar lace plant, *Aponogeton madagascariensis*, is only at home in 20 to 22 °C, slightly acidic water, and is very susceptible to algae infestation.

The beginner is better off not tackling any rare varieties, which are sometimes quite expensive as well, but instead concentrating on species that have proven their value for decades and are so robust that they can tolerate a few beginner's errors. In the following, we'll introduce you to a number of aquatic plants that are hardy and low-maintenance and suitable for every type of aquarium. We distinguish between three main groups:

- Stem plants
- Rosette plants
- Floating plants

The latter group is not of interest for the beginner since they are only used in certain biotope aquariums and for special kinds of fish. They absorb a great deal of light and must be thinned regularly. Among these are plants in the duckweed family (*Lemnaceae*), which are also at home in our own climes, the water ferns (*Salviniaceae*) and the bladderworts (*Lentibulariaceae*).

Stem Plants Look Best in Groups

Among the most popular and widespread aquatic plants are those with a long thin stem and the finest, needle-like leaves. These include the various water milfoils (*Myriophyllum sp.*), available at low cost from plant breeders and at shops, which propagate readily. Water milfoils need to be thinned regularly, because otherwise they will quickly spread out to take over the whole tank, covering the surface of the water.

When planting, take groups of five to six stems at one time and press them lightly into the substrate at the back of the tank, weighing down the roots with some gravel. Otherwise, their air-filled stems will soon cause them to float up to the surface. They quickly put down roots and propagate through side runners. Another plant with fine, dense leaves on flexible stems is the fanwort genus (*Cabomba sp.*), which is at home in the New World. Fanworts, however, place somewhat higher demands on water, light and fertiliser than the milfoils. But when they flourish, they can be a beautiful addition to any tank, especially when they are placed in small groups in the back corners of the aquarium. The most "low-maintenance" of the fanworts is the Carolina Fanwort (*Cabomba caroliniana*). It thrives at temperatures between 20 and 30 °C, pH values from 6.5 to 7.3 and carbonate hardness from 3 to 13 °dH. What it does not appreciate is too much turbulence in the water. It should be kept as far away as possible from airstones or diffusors. Like all *Cabomba*, it loves clear water that is free from suspended particles.

From middle and southern South America, especially from Argentina and the neighbouring countries, a type of frog's bit plant has reached our shores called Brazilian elodea (*Egeria densa*). In its home waters it proliferates so rapidly and densely that it can become a serious problem. In aquariums the plant does particularly well in somewhat harder water and at temperatures around 20 °C. It is thus suitable for cold water tanks, propagating by means of side runners that are simply planted in the substrate, where they soon take root. As with all of the above-named water plants, *Egeria densa* should be planted in the background and along the two short sides of the tank, and trimmed or thinned at regular intervals. Otherwise, you will in no time have a wilderness of vegetation in which there is no longer any room for the fish to swim and not enough light reaching the bottom of the tank.

The acanthus family, sometimes also called "bear's breeches" (*Acanthaceae*), is frequently represented in our aquariums by a few low-maintenance and easy-to-keep varieties. Many of these have slim, elliptical or lancet-shaped leaves, and most thrive under almost all of the usual conditions prevailing in fresh water aquariums. These include *Hygrophilia polysperma*, Indian swampweed or water star, *H. corymbosa*, known as giant hygro, and *H. difformis*, or water wisteria.

All *Hygrophilia* species are quite iron-hungry and must therefore be regularly supplied with liquid fertiliser. Most also appreciate good light and some extra carbon dioxide from time to time. When the leaves become yellow and develop spots, or if the lower leaves fall off or do not grow to the size of the others, these are signs that the pH of the water is too low, in other words, that the water is overly acidic.

To conclude our appraisal of stem plants suitable for beginners' aquariums, we should mention three additional representatives from different families which, with regular iron fertiliser and extra car-

Brazilian elodea (Egeria densa)

Common bladderwort (Utricularia vulgaris)

Star grass (Heteranthera zosterifolia)

Water milfoil (Myriophyllum sp.)

51

*Roseafolia (*Alternanthera reineckii*)*

Indian swampweed or water star

Giant bacopa

bon dioxide, are easy to care for and grow. The first of these is the water hedge (*Didiplis diandra*) from North America, a fine-leaved plant that grows only 12 to 15 cm high and can live in temperatures as low as 20 °C, provided it gets enough light (don't place it under floating or rosette plants).

The second is common hornweed (*Ceratophyllum demersum*), a rootless floating plant, which moves freely through the water. It proliferates rapidly and intensively and must be thinned out often, because it otherwise blocks out the light for other plants growing from the tank bed. In breeding tanks it makes a good place for the young fish to hide, as does the fanwort mentioned above.

The third kind of plant that can enhance the appearance of any tank is the roseafolia (*Alternanthera reineckii*). As the name indicates, this plant is red to red-brown in colour. It has long, lancet-shaped leaves and can grow to about 50 cm high. If it does not get sufficient iron and CO_2, and if the light intensity is too weak, it loses its rustßred colour, but soon regains it if it receives the appropriate fertiliser and more light. This plant makes a lovely contrast to the light green water hyssops (*Bacopa sp.*) and the filigree fanworts.

Eye-Catching Rosette Plants

Fine-leaved, narrow-stemmed plants that look best in small groups form the basic plant stock, so to speak, in most aquariums, building the framework for the aquarium's foliage. But highlights and accents can be set with a whole series of rosette plants, some of which are common and others of which are more rare and highly demanding.

Small species with thin, finger-long leaves can be planted in groups like the stem plants. Larger plants with sturdy, often hand-sized leaves, however, are best as solitaires given pride of place in the foreground. Among the easy-care varieties that are suitable for any tank are several of the arrowheads (*Sagittaria sp.*) from northern America, as well as various exponents of the genus *Vallisneria*, commonly known as eelgrass, ribbon weed or tape grass.

One of these species, *Vallisneria spiralis*, sometimes called corkscrew vallisneria, is at home in southern Europe and North Africa and is well-suited to cold water aquariums. But it also thrives with no problem in warmer water (up to 30 °C). It grows up to 50 cm high and has ribbon-shaped leaves about 5 mm across. It reproduces quickly by sending out run-

Brazilian pennywort (Hydrocotyle leucocephala)

Lizard's tail (Saururus cernuus)

Amazon swordplant (Echinodorus amazonicus)

53

Dwarf crypt (Cryptocoryne x willisii *or* nevillii*)*

Cryptocoryne
pontederiifolia

ners and can sometimes crowd out other less robust plants, especially because it is very tolerant of varying carbonate hardness and pH values.

The above-mentioned arrowheads also make good beginner plants. They have leaves varying from 5 to 30 cm in length, depending on the species, and under the right conditions can form a closed ground cover in the aquarium. It's a good idea to plant them at the back of the tank and leave the foreground open for the popular swordplants (*Echinodorus sp.*), which are among the most coveted aquarium plants. *Echinodorus* is found mainly in tropical and sub-tropical South America, but some varieties—for example *E. cordifolius*—are also found north of Mexico in the warmer regions of North America.

Swordplants usually grow alone and rarely in groups. You would only plant several together in larger aquariums, starting at about 250 litres. *E. amazonicus*, Amazon sword, *E. maior*, ruffled sword and *E. bleheri*, broad leaf Amazon sword grow up to 50 cm high, but usually remain somewhat under that level (aquarium level!). Smaller species, which grow only 15 to 20 cm high, include *E. horizontalis*, horizontal sword, *E. parviflorus*, black sword, and *E. quadricostatus*, dwarf sword. The latter attains a maximum height of 15 cm and can be planted in small groups in the foreground of mid-size to larger aquariums. Although most swordplants come from slightly acidic waters (pH value around 6.5), they also tolerate alkaline water up to pH 7.5. They prefer water temperatures between 22 and 28 °C and carbonate hardness between around 5 and 15 °dH. Many species can make do with relatively little light (40 to 50 W per 100 litres of water), but need regular fertilising with iron and CO_2. The tank bed should not be too densely packed; a mixture of sand and medium quartz gravel (3 to 4 mm) is right for most *Echinodorus* species. They propagate by means of adventitious plantlets that grow out of the flower stalk. You can cut these off and plant them in the bottom of the tank where, given the right conditions, they will put down roots and develop at a leisurely pace.

The arum family (*Araceae*) also offers a few species that can be kept in most aquariums, with very decorative leaves that make an attractive feature. These include the Malayan sword (*Cryptocoryne griffithii siamensis*), which grows to about 20 cm long and 3 cm wide, the *Cryptocoryne crispatula* and a half dozen other *Cryptocoryne* species, which are very tolerant with regard to carbonate hardness, pH values and water temperature. It usually suffices to plant just a few and supply them with iron fertiliser at the beginning. A short time after they take root, they begin to propagate by sending out runners, and in just a few months you will have an even ground cover. If you decide to thin these out and plant some in another tank, you must be careful not to damage the roots. Many of this family tolerate temperatures just over 20 °C, but grow more rapidly and densely at 24 to 26 °C.

Finally, we should not neglect to mention the *Aponogeton* family. Their homeland ranges from Madagascar, to Sri Lanka and India, to Australia. They grow to 20 to 30 cm and at first glance resemble the South American swordplants. But, unlike these, their leaves are usually puckered or ruffled. At water temperatures of 22 °C and over and pH values between 6 and 7.5 they grow quickly and lushly and are hence suitable for larger-sized aquariums. Some species have a dormant period each year during which they lose some leaves and regenerate. This coincides with the dry period in their native habitat, and you just have to be patient during the three or more months it may take before the root tuber develops new shoots.

The beginning aquarium enthusiast will without a doubt find plenty of suitable plants among the above-mentioned stem and rosette varieties to furnish his new tank. In the following we will describe how to plant these in the tank and what kind of care they require.

Planting Your Aquarium

If you're planting an aquarium for the first time, it's a good idea, of course, not to start with the most sensitive and expensive plants, which probably won't live very long, but instead choose the hearty varieties that are tolerant of a few beginner's mistakes. Among both the stem and rosette plants there are a number of robust and long-lasting varieties that grow rapidly and propagate without difficulty. After you have gathered some experience with regard to light intensity, the propagation methods of the various species, fertilising and so forth, you can then try your hand at some of the more challenging plants—always proceeding step by step.

Before you start planting, it's a good idea to first sketch a simplified furnishing and planting plan, showing where the various roots, rocks, technical equipment and plants are to be located in the aquarium. The first elements are a matter of taste, depending on the given conditions (filter, heater, air pump), while the last is a question of plant biology. In other words, the various kinds of plants sharing the tank must share similar requirements. Plants that prefer acidic, soft water cannot be combined well with those that thrive in alkaline, hard water. There is exhaustive literature available on aquatic plants, detailing among other things the most favourable water conditions, the required temperatures and tips for care and maintenance.

For smaller tanks containing up to 100 litres, it's advisable to combine about a half dozen different plant varieties, for example four to five *Hygrophilia difformis* for one of the two back corners, and the same number of *Myriophyllum aquaticum* for the other corner. At left front you could plant a hearty bunch of *Vallisneria spiralis*, which will in time grow along the side panel toward the rear. As the fourth kind of plant you could choose a *Sagittaria subulata* for the front third of the tank, which only grow a few centimetres high and hence don't encroach on the fishes' swimming space. In just a few weeks they form a nice green ground cover in which young and smaller fish feel at home. To add a contrasting colour to

Aponogeton boivinianus

*Giant hygro (*Hygrophilia corymbosa*)*

Planted aquarium

55

Furnishing an aquarium

tion. The most common substrate is fine-grained sand (2 mm grain) and gravel (3 to 5 mm in size). White sand and gravel are visually not as pleasing as brown, yellow or grey. If you obtain your substrate material from a sand bank in a river, you must first wash the materials thoroughly, until the water runs off clear. Finer sand with grains under 1.5 mm is not suitable for an aquarium, because it cannot be adequately aerated and tends to clump together. The tank bed should not under any circumstances contain limestone, as this would continually leach lime into the water and make it too hard—and with the exception of the African cichlids most aquarium fish do not care for hard water. The tank bed should be at least 5 cm deep, somewhat higher at the back than in the front (debris, mulm and mud then collect at the front and can be vacuumed up more easily). Larger tanks—from about 130 to 150 litres—can be divided into one or two terraced sections, with the bed the highest at the rear left or right—up to a depth of 10 to 12 cm. Before layering the bed to its ultimate depth, it's a good idea to distribute a so-called long-term fertiliser among the gravel. This will provide your plants with nutrition for months to come, especially iron, and can be supplemented from time to time.

> **Tip**
> *Stem plants only rarely have roots when purchased. These develop only when the plants have been set into the tank bed. They are planted in groups, but an individual hole is dug for each stalk (at about 1 cm distance from the next one). The bottom leaves should be removed first and not planted into the ground with the stem.*

the green, you might add one or two pots of *Alternanthera reineckii*. With a few *Echinodorus parviflorus*, planted not too close to one another, you can create an aquarium where the fish have plenty of room to swim and there is enough space for you to see them, while the plants have room to grow and spread out.

Arranging the plants

The substrate material you choose for your tank should provide plants with both secure footing and sufficient nutri-

Underwater aquascape

A variety of plants

Don't Crowd the Plants— They Need Space

The next step is to fill the aquarium about one-third to one-half full with water. The plants should be added only once the temperature has reached 20 °C. Plants can be purchased at the fish store, where you will usually find some 40 to 60 different species to choose from. Once home, check the plants for health and get them ready to be arranged. Remove any rotten leaves and cut any bent stems, both sections of which you can then plant. Many rosette plants have bulbs or root tubers, which should be undamaged if the plant is to thrive. Cut back the roots growing out of these until they are a finger's width long, make a hole in the tank bed with your finger and stick the plant in, trying to bend the roots as little as possible. (Tip: try planting them quite deep and then, after covering them with substrate, pulling them up again 1 to 2 cm).

Many plants, particularly the more expensive varieties, are sold in small plastic baskets or clay pots in which they have

Biological equilibrium in the aquarium

Biotope suitable for plants and fish

Gold dust molly

been growing. The former must be removed—using a sharp knife or scissors—and the latter can be set directly into the gravel and removed again if necessary, without having to dig up the plant. One disadvantage here is that the pots might soon become too small for rapidly growing plants and must then be removed.

Aquatic plants cannot be kept out of their element for hours on end, but should be completely submerged in water again as quickly as possible. Otherwise those leaves that were exposed to the air longest will die. You should also take care not to let the water temperature drop below 20 °C and make sure the difference between the water in the aquarium and the water in the transport container is not too stark (+/- 5 °C are acceptable). If the dealer took the plants from a heavily overgrown tank with a thriving snail population, check for snails on the undersides of leaves before putting the plants in your aquarium. If you leave them on the plant, you will soon have your own snail community to contend with, which is not much fun. The eggs are usually about the size of a pinhead, flat, round or oval and brown or brownish black in colour. Carefully scrape them from the leaf and discard.

Once you've arranged all your plants in their designated spots, anchored them in the ground, evened out the bed and are sure that the rocks are in the right place and the roots have been able to take in enough water to weigh them down to the ground, you can carefully fill the rest of the tank with water at the right temperature. For smaller tanks, you can prepare tap water a few days before you'll need it by setting it aside in plastic buckets and adding a water conditioner made for aquarium use. For larger tanks, starting at 150 litres or so, this is not really feasible since hardly anyone is inclined to keep 10 to 15 big plastic buckets full of water around the house for several days. In this case, you can fill the tank with water from the tap—but not colder than 20 °C—and then add water conditioner.

Even though it might be hard to remain patient, the newly furnished and planted aquarium should now be left empty of fish for at least a week, and at best two weeks! Heater, filter, air pump and lighting should be switched on and operating, creating the right conditions for the plants and the fish that are soon to move into their new home. With very little effort, you can have the water values—total and carbonate hardness, pH and CO_2 content—

checked by an expert or an experienced aquarium owner. This will calm any fears you might have and make you confident that your fish will be moving into a biotope where they will feel at home. Once the water values are on target, the plants have put down roots and perhaps grown a bit, the water is clear and odour-free, the heater and pump(s) are operating smoothly, it's time for the big moment: adding the fish (see p. 80 ff.).

Algae—A Nuisance for Every Aquarium Owner

This scene is all too familiar—you've gone to a lot of trouble to set up your tank, installed filter and air pumps, heater and lighting, and purchased expensive plants and fish. The water is crystal clear, the plants are flourishing and the fish are healthy and happy. But after a short time you already notice a very fine, thin film forming on the glass and the plants. These are algae, which both mar the visual splendour of the tank and, when they get out of hand, damage water plants and water quality.

There's no need to take action against natural algae growth. If a tank is in equilibrium, none of the many algae species will proliferate to the extent that it becomes a problem. Green algae (*Chlorophyceae*) even show that the water composition in the aquarium is healthy. But when the algae start to proliferate to the point that they become a nuisance, something must be done. This might involve combating them by mechanical means, i.e. by scraping and vacuuming the glass, or by adding some algae-eating fish to the tank, or as a third measure, only in an emergency, by adding a special anti-algae agent to the water. It also might be helpful to filter any substances suspended in the water (by washing the filter cartridge more often) and to change the water frequently, as well as to ensure a good CO_2 saturation. If you do not succeed at getting the algae under control using one of

the above means and they start to take over the entire tank, the only thing left to do is to start all over again, throwing away the old plants and decorations, such as roots, rocks and snail houses and so on, and replacing them with new ones or boiling them long enough to kill any algae. The filter cartridge must likewise be replaced, and the heating tube and all of the other technical apparatus that comes into contact with the water thoroughly cleaned. And, last but not least, you should try to determine the causes behind the strong algae infestation, because this is always a sign of some sort of imbalance in the aquarium.

Lambchop rasboras and a fighting fish

Algae

Creating Habitats
From Around the World

South American tank

Many beginners just setting up their first tank don't pay much attention to whether the plants and fish they choose might actually be found together in nature. They put together plants and fishes from the most diverse continents and habitats—in accordance with the formula "What's best is whatever looks good to me". There's nothing wrong with this approach, as long as the plants and fish are offered a liveable environment.

In recent years—as our knowledge of the conditions prevailing in nature continues to grow—many aquarium enthusiasts, and not only the old hands, have begun to discover the appeal of the biotope aquarium. This entails the recreation of a habitat that is true to nature, such as one that might be found in the waters of South America, Africa or Asia. You might, for example, reproduce a coastal landscape resembling that of Lake Tanganyika or Lake Malawi (this particular kind of biotope is known as a rocky littoral) and put the corresponding cichlids in the tank. Or one could design an overgrown shore like the ones often found in small, South American tributaries.

Of course, you would then want to add the types of fish that are found naturally in such habitats: certain cichlids, lambchop rasboras (*Rasbora heteromorpha*) or small tetras of the genera *Nannostomus* (pencilfish), *Moenkhausia* and *Hemigrammus*, as well as various catfish species and dwarf cichlids, including the beautiful Borelli's dwarf cichlid (*Apistogramma borelli*) or the three-striped dwarf cichlid (*A. trifasciata*).

Natural Tropical Biotopes and the Beauty of Biotope Aquariums

by Klaus Paysan

Once you have safely put your initial experience with aquariums behind you, probably involving an indiscriminate compilation and mixing up of haphazard fish and plants in one tank, all chosen more or less for their looks alone, you might soon be placing higher demands on the design of your own underwater world. You might fancy a "Dutch tank" put together according to aesthetic considerations, or an extra breeding tank holding just one species and with furnishings expressly designed to accommodate the spawning fish and the raising of young. Or you might be interested in an aquarium displaying, for example, glass fish from various parts of the world, or tanks that reproduce a natural situation from the fishes' native region. This latter kind of tank is known as a biotope aquarium, and these are regarded in specialist circles as the crowning achievement in the world of aquariums.

What is a Biotope?

We humans tend to look at the world through the eyes of a land animal, with the perceptions of a creature whose senses consist of hearing, seeing, touch, smell and taste. But do fish perceive things the same way we do? We can be sure that the fish takes in its surroundings in a way that is vital to its existence.

This means that it is equipped with quite a few more sense organs than we are. While we orient ourselves for the most part with our eyes, and sometimes our ears, the fish has a much wider palette of sensual impressions at its disposal.

With organs in its sides the fish can measure the speed of the current. Taste buds all over its body enable it to recognise food and also the presence of enemies. With electrical organs it can sound out its surroundings using radar, communicate with others of its species using sounds, and bounce signals off objects and measure their echoes like a sonar device. It can perceive chemical differences and heat emanations from a great distance, and it also makes use of the sun's rays, gravity and the pressure conditions at various water depths for orientation. Since all of the fish's sense organs work precisely and are very sensitive to signals all around it, the parameters shaping its biotope are not only those that

we can perceive with our human senses alone. If we try to summarise the physical environment of a fish, which even in larger river areas seems at first to consist only of murky water, we would have to divide this at first glance homogeneous-seeming habitat into a myriad of mountains, deep valleys, current zones, electrical and magnetic fields and various levels of gravity and sunlight. Other properties shaping the biotope include "warm" and "cold" water, the various pH values and inflows, or sources of fresh water. Each of these factors construes a fixed or variable landscape that is clearly recognisable as such for the fish, but which we with our human sense organs cannot begin to perceive.

Therefore, as we have seen, a biotope consists not only of the factors that are immediately perceptible to humans, such as the composition of the ground, the structure and type of plants, light density and heat distribution. Rather, fish biotopes

Borelli's dwarf cichlid

Rainbow fish

Waters rich in tropical fish in India

come from the room's own lamps in the winter months. Then we slowly increase the light intensity using a dimmer on the aquarium lights. This lets the fish slowly wake up. A second lamp then shines much more intensely at various intervals for a total of about four hours each day. With the small halogen lamps available today, we can shine a spotlight on particular areas or plants and increase or vary this light using a dimmer. In addition, we can create areas that are usually in the shade. Since our ornamental fish are primarily native to tropical regions, we can start out with 12 hours of daylight, for example, adding more time if the fishes' natural habitat is from further from the equator, or varying duration and intensity of the lighting according to the season.

Striped krib
(Pelvicachromis taeniatus)

Information

Chemical biotope factors include the pollution of the water with metabolic waste products such as ammoniac, nitrite and nitrate. Ammonia and nitrite are very toxic, while nitrate has a severe impact on the growth and aggressiveness of the fish and on their timidity and fearfulness. These influences can be controlled through buffering via the mulm, ion exchangers (e.g. through clay in the tank bed) and especially by regularly exchanging the water.

are characterised by the constantly changing composition of the water, light and temperature. How can we influence this watery biotope, something which is virtually invisible to us, in such a way that our fish feel at home there?

Light and Lighting

In the morning we let the muted daylight slowly enter the room—it might

Chemical Factors

The chemistry in an aquarium already changes with the amount of light. With the assimilation of carbon dioxide by the plants and the resulting production of atomic oxygen, the pH value sinks steeply toward more acidic values. As soon as the light intensity lessens, the plants produce less oxygen and the pH value tends more in the alkaline direc-

Whiptail catfish
(Sturisoma festivum)

tion. We can also adjust the oxygen content and carbon dioxide concentration further with the air pump. The more air bubbles, the more carbon dioxide is being forced out of the water and the less the plants can assimilate in order to produce oxygen. But carbon dioxide, atomic oxygen (i.e. nascent oxygen) and molecular oxygen have major effects in stimulating various fish behaviours and the growth of plants, algae and micro organisms. The relationships between these diverse factors can work to stimulate spawning; growth processes as well as embryo development times are also affected.

Temperature

The simplest and most natural method of creating a natural temperature range is to switch off the heater at night. Since our normal room temperature is usually about 20 to 21 °C, this does not lead to a dangerous drop in the tank's water temperature. On the other hand, if you have nocturnal fish such as catfish, then your tank should not be cooler at night.

Another method for structuring temperature to mimic natural conditions is to heat certain parts of the tank, in particular by means of supplementary heating periods during which an extra lamp also provides additional light. There are diverse ways of doing this, with varying results: heat can for example be provided evenly by laying a heating pad under the aquarium. A heating tube can be laid on the floor of the tank along an edge or in the middle. It can be hung vertically in a corner, in the stream of filtered water or in the air bubbling up from the air pump, or in a still area of the tank.

The heating pad, or a styrofoam panel underneath the tank, can help to ensure an even temperature throughout the tank, as can a quite strong flow of filter water through the aquarium. Water cur-

rents can exert a substantial influence on a biotope. Variations in the direction and speed of flow and the concentration of the water jet can lead to different structures emerging in the aquarium. This offers a wide field for experimentation, with the hope that we will ultimately be able to create an overall biotope that is highly agreeable to the fish in our tank.

Different Fish— Different Living Habits

Before we begin to set up a biotope aquarium, it is particularly important to first know something about the fishes' living habits. A fish that lurks in wait for prey will appreciate strong directional water currents a great deal less than a school fish whose usual habitat is a mountain stream. Natives of a sluggishly flowing but deep rainforest stream will respond to a nightly temperature drop of more than 2 °C with displeasure, if not with increased susceptibility to sickness. Intensive supplementation with carbon dioxide can prove fatal if, during the night, the plants have stopped assimilating and are in a dissimilation phase instead, using up the available oxygen and giving off even more carbon dioxide.

Dwarf or golden otocinclus (Otocinclus affinis)

Information

*In order to stimulate
reproduction in many
species, a warm or
cool tropical rainfall
can be simulated using
a watering can filled
with rainwater-like,
low-saline water.
This changes the
aquarium biotope in
a way that is typical
for the tropical home
waters of our orna-
mental fish. Up until
this point we have
not addressed the
geological and
vegetation-related
limitations that are
also important com-
ponents of a biotope,
and which can also
be reproduced in
our aquariums. The
construction of the
aquarium using the
right ground cover,
stones, roots and
plants is just as impor-
tant for the fish as
the virtually invisible
factors described
above.*

*Rio Negro,
Amazon biotope*

Another extremely important aspect of the biotope is the kind of food the fish are given and how this food is provided. A fish from rapidly flowing water expects to have to catch its food, so the best way to feed this kind of fish with frozen or flaked food is to distribute the food in the water with your fingers.

An even better and more natural method is to provide live feed that must be caught. Many catfish look for food scattered on the bottom of the tank and some breeds wait in ambush until their prey swims right past them. But what would never happen to a fish in nature is the conventional way fish are fed by the busy aquarium owner: the food always comes at the same time, and is always the same and in overabundance. A few days of fasting have frequently proven quite favourable, in particular when fish that have grown fat refuse to spawn. What's not good for fish is adding chemicals to the water. The chemistry of the aquarium can only be changed when the water is replaced — but that makes for an abrupt change for the fish. For some kinds of fish, in particular those, which were captured in the wild rather than bred in captivity, the water in the tank should be exchanged only drop by drop.

Rapid temperature changes by more than 5 °C should also be avoided in order not to endanger fish that are weakened or already ailing.

A Natural Biotope for our Ornamental Fishes

The Amazon and its tributaries in the tropical rainforest, the Lower Niger, Zaire, and the great rivers of Southeast Asia

These waters are usually brown in colour and rich in humic acid. Tributaries are often fed by rapidly flowing mountain streams and rivers, which bring the products of erosion with them, often leading to considerable chemical differences between source and tributary. The temperatures and oxygen content of these river legs are also often quite different from those in the main river. The confluences often flow quite gradually into the main stream, and only after a long period of time is the equalisation of the existing differences complete. At the bottom of the stream there are springs that are quite rich in mineral content, which we can sometimes see as long plumes running upward through the water (e.g. due to a different colour or different temperature). With their broader spectrum of sense organs, fish readily recognise these differences as a clearly structured underwater landscape. At the surface, immense changes take place every day owing to the strong tropical rainfall. Temperature, pH value and oxygen content at the surface fluctuate widely throughout the day. In addition, the assimilation process of the algae in the sunlight enriches the water with oxygen.

For long stretches along their shores the rivers are lined with overhanging trees, which often plunge them into deep shadow. Large air roots, reed-filled zones and fallen trees with their upturned roots also structure this biotope, along with washed-out banks, deep caves, holes and shallow bays.

The great rivers are interrupted here and there by geological thresholds. Waterfalls and cataracts strongly augment the oxygen concentration. These turbulent points are where an especially large number of

Bleeding-heart tetra

Siamese fighting fish

Ram cichlid

fish accumulate, since there are often a wide variety of biotopes within a short distance of one another.

Streams in the moist savannah, the Upper Niger and Upper Nile

These streams are often accompanied by gallery forests or extended reed zones. Because of strong sunlight, the temperature differences at the surface are well-structured, as are those between shallow and deep areas and between water surface and deep-flowing currents. During the monsoon period the rivers in the source regions swell and flood wide areas, which because of their shallowness are then warmed up by the sun and cool off just as strongly at night. Only when the monsoon reaches the territory in which the stream is located do the clouds then prevent major fluctuations in temperature. The tropical rains change the chemical composition of the river water, which has a much higher mineral content in the dry period but is also subject to less fluctuation.

The surface water, especially that located above shallow underwater sand dunes, is very low in microbes due to the strong UV rays of the sun, while in the flood areas the rotting land vegetation with its typical hay infusion fauna is an ideal breeding ground for young fish. These often immense shallow flood areas are cut off from the main stream during the dry period and then become very warm biotopes for millions of fish. The fish then live off the larvae of mosquitoes and gnats, but they themselves become prey for the numerous cranes, water and wading birds, as well as the larger predatory fish.

The beds of the main streams are often pebbly, in the lower areas sandy and in the flood zones and reed belts muddy and clayey, frequently covered with rotting plant material. In the flood regions water lilies flourish, as does Ottelia and other plants whose bulbs or tubers have survived the dry period undamaged.

Tropical lakes and standing waters

If you wish, you can closely recreate various biotopes in your aquarium. You might choose, for example, Lake Malawi with its extensive rocky littoral, one shore consisting of gigantic rounded granite blocks plunging precipitously into the depths. Algae grow on the stone surfaces under the water's surface, serving as a source of food for many fish. Some species have a protruding lower jaw with fine, grater-like teeth to scrape off the

Tropical water lily

Water hyacinth

*Variatus platyfish
(Xiphophorus variatus)*

African lakeshore biotope

algae. The water surface is often churned up by strong winds, while in the deeper layers there is very little movement. The surface water is rich in oxygen, and the lake is on the whole quite high in minerals and hence alkaline. There is strong sunshine in the daytime, which is only dampened by cloud cover in the monsoon period.

Similar conditions prevail in the similarly saline Lake Tanganyika. There the waves are even stronger, and the many rock crevices make good hiding places for the cichlids. There is often sandy ground in the bays between the rocks, and out in the open areas great schools of fish can be found.

The vast Lake Victoria, on the other hand, is relatively still and has a number of islands. Its shores consist to a great extent of reed and papyrus swamps, and many islands of reed and papyrus float on the lake.

Malawi blue cichlid

Tropical forest streams

The streams in tropical forests are usually clear, low in salt and coloured yellow to brown by humic acid. They have a low pH value. The shores are often hollowed out under the roots of the gallery trees, creating large, dark overhangs and deep holes to make homes for numerous species of catfish and provide shelter for other kinds of fish. The ground is often made up of fine sand and usually covered with dark leaves. In the open areas that receive more light, there are carpets of water lilies. Grasses and branches hang into the water, and broad-leaved plants such as the Anubias grow over and under the water's surface. Since in the tropical rainforest it rains almost every day year-round and the air temperature varies by only a few degrees, the fish here are very sensitive to fluctuations in water quality and temperature.

Brooks in savannah regions

The inhabitants of savannah brooks are accustomed to completely different conditions. The seasons are divided starkly into monsoon periods and dry stretches when the streams might even dry up completely. In monsoon season there are heavy thunderstorms, the current swells into rapids, whole sections of the shore are washed away and the water landscape can change completely in the space of a few minutes. The pH value, mineral content and concentration of toxins in the

Victoria Lake in East Africa

Rainbow fish

water are also totally different in the different seasons. The temperature change from day to night is considerable, and rainfall can also sink temperatures in the brooks by several degrees within a short time. The stream bed often consists of pebbles and sand, and in the deeper hollows also of dark mud, which in the dry period often decomposes to form a stinking mass. Some brooks are framed by gallery forests, in which case they are very well shaded. However, the fish still have the optportunity to swim to nearby sunny areas.

One Fish, Many Different Biotopes

As we can see, nature tends to shape the biotope characteristics that we can perceive in a similar fashion all over the world, and the factors necessary for the well-being of the fish often lie in areas that have little to do with the form of the ground or surroundings, nor with the type of plants. The main characteristics shaping a biotope are light, pH value, the mineral content of the water and the currents running through it. In the case of breeding fish, the seasonal fluctuations in these latter factors also play a major role.

To give you an idea of the variety of biotopes experienced by one fish species, consider that fish change biotopes with the seasons. They even seek out a different biotope in the daytime than the one they inhabit at night. We can take a small step toward recreating this diversity by choosing tanks of adequate size. The minimum size should be 80 cm long, and in tanks holding 15 litres of water or more it should not be difficult to establish a stable relationship between water conditions, mineral concentration, microbes and algae, and plants and fish. This is the only way to create a satisfying semblance of their home waters to please both ourselves and the fish.

Setting up a Biotope Tank

The first thing to find out is whether the fish you are interested in prefer water low in salt and acidic, or hard and alkaline. This is the criterion by which you will choose your decorative stones for the aquarium. In both cases, the sand and

Decorative granite stones

Decorative roots

Shore biotope

gravel used should be river sand that is neutral and low in lime. River sand is not as sharp-edged as sand taken from quarries. Fish that bottom-feed and burrow in the ground, such as corydoras and loaches, might easily injure themselves on sharp quartz pebbles. Today, there is a wide variety of gravel available in different colours. It's best to purchase a few different colours, ranging from light yellow to dark or black. Then you can emphasize the shaded parts of the aquarium even more strongly with dark gravel. This in turn will prompt many fish to show their colours even more strongly.

Be careful that the stones you choose to decorate the tank are not too heavy and that no sharp corners are pressing into the glass at the bottom of the tank. If necessary, you can lay down a thick styrofoam sheet underneath. For fish that prefer hard water, you can choose almost any kind of stones, but for soft-water fish, it's best to first do a hydrochloric acid test. Just a drop on the stone is sufficient. If the stone begins to foam, this means it contains lime and is not suitable for soft-water fishes. But be careful: hydrochloric acid is a dangerous chemical! Avoid any contact with skin or clothing—or with the water in the tank!

Designing a biotope using stones, wood and styrofoam

There are plenty of interesting rocks and stones to choose from at the pet shop. But you can also look for them on the shores of rivers or streams, or see what you can find at the shop of a stonemason who makes gravestones. Not too many stones should be crowded into a single tank—that can look artificial and tacky. The pebbles on the tank bed, however, can come from different regions and be multi-coloured, just like in nature.

You also must exercise some care in choosing wood ornaments. The wood must be fossil or semi-fossil wood from moors, the organic components of which have already decomposed. It's best to soak the wood first for at least a week in hot water, in order to remove any possible toxins. Fossilised oak pieces in particular, which are often available in many decorative shapes and sizes in stores, give off a great deal of tannic acid that may sour the water and turn it an intense yellow colour. This is not only unattractive, but can also be fatal to the fish.

A scenic backdrop to the aquarium can be formed using wood pieces, thick vegetation and also deeply creviced styrofoam pieces painted with non-toxic brown paint. Or, you can evoke the illusion of the sea receding into the distance with a styrofoam panel painted in shades of blue and sea green, which, unlike the thick styrofoam used to simulate part of the shoreline, is mounted outside the aquarium.

Some Types of Biotope Aquariums

The North American shore biotope

This is one of the few biotopes that can be recreated without difficulty in a smaller tank. The fish are happy with room temperatures as low as 10 °C, and they also tolerate wide fluctuations in water hardness. The bed can be made up of river pebbles in various colours, rising up toward the back of the tank and falling off in one corner. The air pump can be placed there, and the mulm will naturally settle and can be easily vacuumed up. The sand between the pebbles can be planted with North American plants such as *Ludwigia*, American water hedges (*Didiplis diandra*), hairgrass (*Eleocharis*) and dwarf corkscrew vallisneria (*Vallisneria spiralis*). Pygmy sunfishes (*Elassoma*) and mosquitofish (*Heterandria formosa Girard*) will feel right at home among these plants, especially if the area is divided into several territories by larger pebbles. These fish from the southern littoral of North America do not like a strong current.

To clean the tank, direct a current through the low-lying areas every 14 days in the direction of the rear, deeper corner.

The European cold water biotope

One of the main problems with this biotope is the temperature. It must be as low as possible, for the benefit both of the fish and the plants. The tank can be divided diagonally. On one side is the open swimming area over a bed of coarse river pebbles and large rounded stones. We then run a filter jet from the front to the back corner, so that the entire half is quite turbulent. The other half is the still water zone in which pond and water lilies growing above fine sand line the front panel.

This kind of tank is good for loaches, minnows, sticklebacks and other Euro-

School of minnows

pean coldwater fish. These fish often must be kept in schools, necessitating a strong filter to keep the tank clean and to create a strong current.

A biotope for live-bearing toothed carp from the tropical Americas

These fish love hard water, so any kind of stones can be used to furnish their home. The sandy ground can be planted with a carpet of small vallisneria, sagittaria and large floating grasses. As a centrepiece we can use an echinodorus. For nibbling and as a hiding place for the young, arrange water nymphs, ceratophyllum and elodea close together at the back corners, leaving open space at midtank and at the top for the fish to swim around. This is a good environment for guppies, swordtails and various mollies. To make sure food scraps get eaten, populate the nether regions with corydoras, and add a few bristlenose plecos (*Ancistrus)* to keep algae growth in check.

A rocky littoral with porous limestone

For fish from the alkaline, saline lakes of East Africa, we can use porous limestone to create a landscape with several clearly

and smaller females. Caves that become narrow at the back or small rock crevices can often save lives. In an aquarium heavily populated with species of varying colours, the existence of numerous hiding places ensures that the unavoidable fights will end without incident. Strong filters are needed due to the size of the fish and the resulting accumulation of excrement. Strong, even alternating, currents rushing through the rocky fissures are very stimulating for the fish. The uppermost stones should be intensely illuminated so that a thick carpet of algae forms to feed the algae-eaters. The plants chosen should be quite hearty and inedible, such as java fern (*Microsorum pteropus*), puckered cryptocorynes, or giant vals (*Vallisneria gigantea*), but even then you can't be sure that they won't one day fall victim to the rapacious fish. For food and oxygen add some free-floating hornwort (*Ceratophyllum demersum*) or water nymph (*Najas*). The rocks must be carefully laid and wedged in tightly, because cichlids like to burrow, and collapsing rock landscapes can easily break the glass.

South and Central American aquarium; fancy guppies (Poecelia reticulata)

defined territories. The cichlids from these waters are very aggressive, so we need to provide several shelters for young fish

Flat Asiatic lake landscape

This is an absolute soft-water community with barbs living in thick vegetation. The ground is sandy to muddy with numerous roots and branches, and there are legions of types of plants. However, we must leave some free swimming space in the middle, surrounding by large-leaved floating plants. More delicate plants can be arranged in groups, serving as food, spawning grounds and a hiding place for the young. Barbs are peaceful school fish, and quite lively. They can form a dense population and tend to overeat; thus they should only be fed when hungry. The aquarium needs strong filtration and frequent water changes. Carbon dioxide fertiliser is a good idea to keep the plants healthy. At night artificial aeration is then required to prevent CO_2 build-up.

Asiatic pond landscape

This is the natural biotope of the labyrinth fishes: densely planted vegetation on a dark ground with several pieces of wood and roots, and numerous floating plants which must frequently be thinned out in order to leave some open space on the water's surface. Large-leaved plants with low light requirements can be planted in the bed. The current meanders leisurely through these ground plants, while the upper areas should remain relatively still. Labyrinth tanks should also have a cover so the fish do not catch cold when they come up for air.

The plants must not be fertilised with carbon dioxide because the fish would otherwise be poisoned by the carbonation that is building up on the water's surface. Labyrinth fish can sometimes be quite aggressive, so it's advisable to keep species with varying colouration and patterns together in the aquarium. For breeding you will need to keep some space free at the surface and have several feathery-leaved water plants for the smaller fish to use, in which they can build their nests.

African stream bank

Here, we burn the features of a steep riverbank into a thick styrofoam panel, and set into it hard-leaved plants such as anubias. At the front there should be plenty of open swimming space over a bed covered with coarse river pebbles and sand in which single long-leaved Cape lilies (*Crinum x powellii*) and large-leaved anubias are growing. Boughs and fossilised wood add structure to the tank's floor. Red cichlids are the right species for this tank. They are known for their extreme aggressiveness, which is, however, subject to individual variation. Often, pairs can be peaceful even well after spawning. The safest approach is to raise a large number of young fish all together and then choose harmonious

pairs for breeding. Strong filtration and currents in the open swimming area along the front panel corresponds to the conditions found in nature.

Ram cichlid

Water corkscrew or common vallisneria

A Brief ABC
of Fish Food

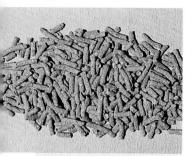

Granulated feed for catfish

Feed tablets for all ornamental fish

Fish as feed

Fish and shrimp (predatory fish feed)

Platys eating from feed tablet

Apart from providing a suitable home for our ornamental fish, giving them the right food is another important factor for their well-being and health. The science of fish food has made major strides during the past three decades and today we are able to provide appropriate, nutritious food for almost any species of fish that finds its way into European aquariums. Just a few years ago it was quite difficult to keep some cichlid varieties, because there was no food on the market suitable for this breed. But by now there are various feeds on the market that contain all of the necessary elements, such as carbohydrates, proteins, fats, fibre, minerals and vitamins, to help cichlids live long, healthy lives and bear young.

And yet, although machine-made and industrially produced feed fulfils almost all of our ornamental fishes' needs, there is one element missing. From our knowledge of more highly developed vertebrates, mammals and birds, we know that searching for and consuming food is not just a matter of nutrition, but also forms a pleasurable pastime for animals, and an important part of their lives. This is probably also the case for fish. Our aquarium inhabitants live in a kind of artificial land of plenty. They have no enemies and must rarely stake out territories and defend them from adversaries; they enjoy ideal water conditions in the tank and regularly receive food with no effort on their part. By taking the correct approach to feeding, however, we can try to keep the fish active and still make sure they are getting all the nutrients they need.

Dry, Freeze-dried and Live Feed

How does the old saying go? "God has to accommodate a variety of boarders". This also holds true for our aquariums. Some of our fish are herbivores, others carnivores, and others still are omnivores. Vegetarian diets are provided almost exclusively in the form of dry food flakes, i.e. food that is required by law to contain less than 14 % water. With this low water content the food does not provide a fit environment for fungus or bacteria and hence keeps much longer

than fresh food. One disadvantage of dry food is that the vitamins added to it can lose their potency over time. Therefore, it's a good idea to buy food with the latest possible expiration date.

Dry food can also be purchased in the form of pellets (pressed food in various shapes and sizes), granulates, sticks or tablets. All of these forms contain vegetable ingredients such as soy and cereal flour, vegetables and various greens, as well as animal ingredients for omnivores such as egg and milk powder, fishmeal, ground krill and shrimp. Dry food is scattered or laid in the aquarium, or can sometimes be stuck on the glass in the form of a tablet. The fish then pick and pinch off small pieces until the chunk of food is wholly consumed or falls to the ground.

Some fish eat mostly or exclusively a vegetarian diet and like to eat green vegetables. Among these species are the Siamese algae eater (*Crossocheilus siamensis*), the common pleco (*Hypostomus punctatus*), the sailfin molly (*Poecilia velifera*) and the Chinese algae eater or sucking loach (*Gyrinocheilus aymonieri*). You can feed them with well-cleaned and briefly parboiled salad and spinach, dandelion leaves and even some fresh beech leaves. For your bottom feeders, you can place the food on the ground, weighing it down with a stone. After five or six hours at the latest, however, you should remove what's left from the tank. Special plant flakes can also be used instead of fresh greens.

Dry Food Spoils Rapidly in the Tank

Food that sinks to the bottom of the tank without being eaten is one of the biggest problems in keeping ornamental fish. Fish other than the bottom feeders, such as catfish and loaches, do not eat food once it has reached the ground, meaning that the food then spoils rapidly and pollutes the water. It is therefore very important not to give the fish too much food at once, but instead to spread three or four smaller portions throughout the day. You should also include some fish in the tank that are bottom feeders and will search out and consume the food that lands on the tank floor.

For fish that eat both plant and animal foods, there is dry food available that contains both. It is usually well accepted by the omnivores—all the more since most ornamental fishes come from generations of domestic breeding. Fish caught in the wild sometimes refuse to eat flakes or tablets and have to be given live feed; with a little patience, however, they can often be gradually accustomed to flakes over the course of a few weeks or months.

Predatory Fish Need Live Feed

Many species can be classified as predators since their diet consists almost exclusively of other animals. In nature these fish hunt and consume living water and airborne insects and their larvae (which often develop in water, such as the many mosquito species), along with worms,

Chinese algae eater (Gyrinocheilus aymonieri)

Animal feed scientist

Garnet tetras
(Hemigrammus pulcher)

but today the selection is much larger. There are scuds and water fleas, and a whole host of tiny arthropods such as daphnia, bosmina and cyclops, which can be fished out of standing ponds and pools in the summer months using an extremely fine-meshed scoop. Other live feed includes black, white and red mosquito larvae, as well as infusorians, a catch-all term for all of the microscopic one-celled and larger creatures, which are useful especially to feed fish young. Unfortunately, there isn't an adequate supply of live feed the whole year round, meaning you will have to resort to freeze-dried or frozen feed from time to time, which not all fish will accept. It's therefore a good idea to accustom the fish during the summer to freeze-dried or frozen feed (which of course must be thawed before feeding!). This can be done by simply mixing it in with the live feed, slowly raising the proportion of non-fresh to fresh.

krill, rotifers and other micro organisms that are often only 0.15–0.3 mm long! It used to be possible to purchase only tubifex and whiteworms at the pet shop,

Freezing Mosquito Larvae and Krill

It's also possible, of course, to freeze your own live feed during the summer, when it's available in greater abundance and is thus less expensive than in winter. You can freeze mosquito larvae, krill (*Artemia*) and water fleas—as well as tubifex and whiteworms—in varying portion sizes. The plastic bags you can buy for making ice cubes are ideal for medium-sized portions that, once thawed, can be used up in one or two days. Another method is to freeze the feed in thin plastic freezer bags, pressing out the air to form a layer that is between 2 and 3 mm thick. Once this layer is frozen, you can break or hack off pieces in the desired portion size and put the rest back into your freezer. Some of your family members might of course not be so keen on having frozen mosquito larvae and krill sharing freezer space with their beef fillets and fish sticks!

Walking catfish (Clarias Batrachus)

Common pleco or sucker catfish
(Hypostomus punctatus, Liposarcus
multiradiatus *or* pardalis *and others*)

Once feed has been thawed, it should under no circumstances be refrozen, and it should not be kept in the refrigerator for longer than about 36 hours. With some experience you will know how much frozen feed you need to thaw to make sure your aquarium guests have just enough, but not too much, to eat.

Freeze-dried feed (e.g. krill, water bugs, mosquito larvae, scuds and fish pieces) does not, of course, require refrigeration. However, many fish refuse to eat it—and then you will have to try the other varieties of feed.

When, How Often and How Much to Feed?

In nature fish are usually occupied for much of the day with searching for food and consuming it. In the aquarium, how-ever, they get so much food at one time that a maximum of one to two feedings per day suffices. If you are feeding only once a day, then put the dry or live feed into the tank in the morning; this gives the fish plenty of time to consume it. If you feed twice a day, then the last feeding should take place at least one hour before the light goes out in the aquarium, since most fish do not eat in the dark and the food will otherwise sink to the ground and spoil. Young fish need four to eight feedings per day—and this is only possible if you stay home the whole day and continually check on them. If you are not giving the fish live feed, you can purchase an electrically operated automatic feeder and program it to release a certain amount of flakes or tablets into the water several times a day. Some models can be set for up to 14–28 days and are thus extremely practical for holidays.

With regard to food quantity, as we have mentioned several times above, it is better to give your aquarium inhabitants just enough rather than too much. But how can you tell what amount is just enough? Do the following experiment: put a pinch of food in the water and watch to see how long it takes the fish to consume this amount completely. If the food is consumed within minutes and the fish are still looking for more, the amount was either just enough or not enough. So put another pinch in. If some of the food now falls to the ground without being consumed, it was too much and the amount should be reduced accordingly. After just a few days you will have a feeling for what is enough and what is too much. If the population of your tank changes, you will of course have to adjust the amount as required.

If you plan to go away for a weekend, there's no need to ask the neighbours to feed your fish. The animals can easily go two to three days without food. If you are raising young, however, it's always better to stay home and keep a close eye on them.

Tip
Even if you usually give your fish the same kind of food, it's nice to spoil them from time to time with a special treat. This might be dried insects or krill, mosquito larvae, so-called species-appropriate food (e.g. food especially designed for cich-lids, carnivores or toothed carp), colour-enhancing food, or food for growing fish, for herbivores or for species that require special nutrients (for example, spawning fish). The same goes for fish as for humans—variety is the spice of life. Keep in mind that even dry food does not keep forever. Flakes and tablets should be used up within one year or replaced. They should be stored in a cool, dry place and not exposed unnecessarily to bright light (which leads to vitamin loss).

uying and Introducing Fish Into Their New Home

Purchased fish are transported in a plastic bag

At the pet shop

Once the aquarium is furnished and planted, has been left to run for a week or two, and no problems have been encountered, it's finally time to begin introducing fish. You have certainly already devoted some thought to what kinds of ornamental fish you would like to have, and how many will feel comfortable in your tank. There is a simple rule of thumb to determine this number: calculate 1 cm fish per 1 litre of water—as long as the aquarium is well-planted, filtered and aerated.

For a 100-litre tank this means about 25 fish measuring 4 cm in length, such as the popular neon tetra (*Paracheirodon innesi*) or the equally widespread beginner fish, the flame tetra (*Hyphessobrycom flammeus*). A few of the other low-maintenance species are somewhat larger: the lovely rosy barb (*Barbus conchonius*) reaches a length of between 12 and 14 cm in its natural habitat, but usually stays under 10 cm in aquariums. About a dozen of these alone would already fill the above-mentioned 100-litre tank!

Quite a bit smaller are the usually easy-care live-bearing toothed carp species such as the swordtails (*Xiphophorus helleri*), platys (*Xiphophorus maculatus*) and mollies (*Poecilia sphenops*). The females of these species grow to about 6 cm long and the males to about 4 cm. About 20 to 30 fish of this size can be kept in a 100-litre tank.

Not all fish species spend their time in the same parts of the tank. There are some that spend all or almost all of their time on the ground, and others that are known as surface fish because of their habit of keeping to the upper third or fourth of the tank.

The great majority of fish, however, prefer the middle area of the aquarium. When discussing the various species later on we will indicate which part of the tank the fish prefer so you can put together your fish wish list in such a way that fish from all three regions are included. But the advice of a knowledgeable friend or dealer cannot be replaced by even the best of books.

Bringing Your New Friends Home—and Quickly!

Before taking a decision to buy one species or another, find out through reading—or from knowledgeable friends and experts—about the habits and needs of the fish in question, approximately how big the fish will be as adults (remember: 1 cm of fish per litre of water) and which food they require. It makes sense not to buy all the fish you would like to have at your first visit to the pet shop, but instead to fill the tank to capacity bit by bit. Once you've decided what kind of fish you want, you can pick out the individual fish in the store's tank—provided the large number of fish they keep there doesn't make this impracticable.

Make sure you choose the largest and most lively specimens, with intense colouring and no sunken "hungry stomachs". The dealer will catch the fish with a scoop and put them in a plastic bag that's half-filled with water, tying the bag up for transport. The oxygen in the upper part of the bag will be adequate for the fish to get by for a few hours, so you need not worry that they might suffocate in the bag.

Nonetheless, whether it's summer or winter: make your way home with your fish as quickly as possible. In summer take care that the bag is not sitting somewhere in the car where it is exposed to direct sunlight, and in winter make sure the water doesn't get too cold. Both of these dangers can be easily prevented by wrapping the plastic bag in newspaper or a towel. If it's very cold outside, it will be best to put the bag in a small, well-insulated styrofoam container, where the water temperature will remain relatively constant for a long period of time.

*Copper tetra (*Hasemania melanura*)*

Putting new fish in the tank

Guppy tank

even out once the bag has been floating in the tank for a while. If there is little difference in temperature you can mix the water together, i.e. add one or two cups of water from the aquarium to the transport bag and repeat the procedure at two-minute intervals. If the fish show no abnormal reaction, for example swimming frantically to and fro, gasping for air or even going belly up in the water, you can now carefully pour the contents of the bag into the aquarium and then let your small friends swim out into their new home.

For one or two days you should leave them in peace, not giving them any food and especially not tapping on the glass or sticking your hand in the water. The fish have to get used to their new environment and will often hide at first in the vegetation or behind some of the roots and stones. If you later introduce new fish of the same species that are already living in the tank, you have to watch carefully to see if the old residents are going after or injuring the new ones. Some species are quite territorial, especially during breeding time, and do not tolerate any fish of the same gender and kind in their midst.

Most aquarium owners, however, have only one tank and must therefore sometimes bring new fish home and have them move in with the established residents of the tank. This always entails a certain amount of risk: the old fish or new fish might be sick and infect the healthy ones. Experienced fish owners who have rare and expensive species living in their tanks will therefore always put new fish in a quarantine tank for three to four weeks and closely observe whether they show any unusual reactions, behaviour or physical abnormalities. If this is not the case, they can then be transferred into the community or single-species tank (a community tank is made up of several unrelated fish species, while a single-species tank holds just one kind of fish, which are usually school fishes).

Quarantine Tanks for Rare and Expensive Species

Once at home, the fish should immediately be put into the prepared tank, plastic bag and all. If the temperature difference between the aquarium water and the bag of fish is extreme, it will

With a Little Luck You'll Soon Have Offspring in the Tank

Robust and low-maintenance fish, especially some members of the toothed carp family, are easy to breed—think only of the proverbially prolific guppy (*Poecilia reticulata*). The female can give birth to up to 150 young in only four to six weeks. If this takes place in a well-populated community tank, the brood will usually serve the adult fish as live feed and will rarely survive beyond a brief youth! Other toothed carp, the egg layers, spawn and then forget all about their eggs; these can be moved into a breeding tank where they will develop further on their own.

In the next chapter, book author Helmut Stallknecht will report on the necessary conditions for breeding and how the beginner can breed low-maintenance species that do not require any special preparation, such as a higher water temperature, changes in the water chemistry, or special feed. Once you have gathered some experience with these low-maintenance species, you can later try your hand at breeding the more demanding and sensitive varieties. But keep in mind that you will then need several breeding tanks and a certain amount of knowledge about water composition—for example, pH, CO_2, carbonate and total hardness. This knowledge can be obtained from the diverse literature available, however, with a little effort. And thanks to the test sets and chemical agents that are available at every pet shop, you can very soon put what you've learned into practice.

Nevertheless, the beginner who has a tank full of 20–30 fish will be especially proud if she wakes up one morning to discover a swarm of newborn guppies or swordtails frolicking in her aquarium.

Pearl gourami
*(*Trichogaster leeri*)*

Lemon tetra (Hyphessobrycon pulchripinnis)

Glowlight tetra (Hemigrammus erythrozonus)

Ornamental Fish Breeding
Made Easy

*Three-striped pencilfish
(Nannostomus
trifasciatus)*

Developing fish embryo

by Helmut Stallknecht

We All Started Out Small

Whereas caring for the readily available varieties of aquarium fish is hardly a problem as long as one observes a few important principles, breeding these exotic species is still widely thought to be a complicated undertaking. Many people believe that carefully orchestrated water compositions, ultra-hygienic breeding tanks and highly sophisticated methods are required to prompt fish to produce offspring. However, even today's successful breeding specialists once started out with species that were easy to breed, which produced offspring spontaneously. After a number of such successes, they felt confident enough to try breeding species that are considered more finicky, and discovered certain methods that lead to success.

Above all, it is important to observe the fish closely. You need to focus on certain characteristics that show whether you even have pairs, i.e. males and females, among the fish in your tank. When you first stock your aquarium, it will probably be with young fish, and you can't necessarily tell until they mature whether they are males or whether they will retain the female colouring that is typical of young fish, as well. Even aquarium owners who

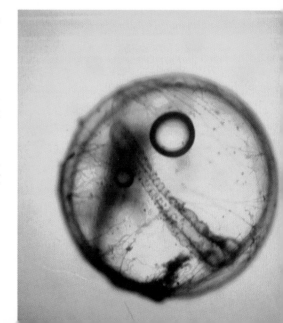

do not have their hearts set on breeding should try to make sure they have both males and females in the tank. Having both genders simply makes for a more interesting aquarium. In most species it is only the males who display intense colouring, and they are always more colourful than the females. The males' fins can also grow much larger than those of females in some cases. But it would be wrong to keep only males, because this could lead to battles ending in injury or even the untimely demise of the underdogs.

Harmony is Short-lived

In addition to the endless variety in body types, colouring and fins, each kind of fish also has its own behavioural patterns, which might very well lead to conflicts in the small space defined by the aquarium walls. Even young fish jostle one another playfully—but with advancing reproductive maturity their battles gradually become more serious. In nature, males must be able to defend a territory at least during spawning time; this is an absolute prerequisite for successful reproduction. You might not have planned for this when you set up your aquarium and purchased your first young fish, but... It usually takes about three months before the more serious wrangling begins.

The harmony prevailing up until then can be lost when one fish starts trying to lord it over part of the aquarium, or perhaps the entire tank, and begins to chase the other fish around. They have no place to escape, get bitten and injured, and finally the troublemaker is removed so that peace can reign once more. Perhaps this is really the case for a few days, but it won't be long before the next fish tries to become the kingpin as he no longer has any rivals and wants to stake out his own territory for breeding preparations. This is completely normal and part of the biological development process of almost all species of fish.

Courtship and Mating in the Community Tank

Conditions in community aquariums—where many fish species are often kept that would not share a living space in nature—can often lead to inter-species conflicts as each kind of fish attempts to live out its biologically programmed devel-

Bleeding-heart tetra (Hyphessobrycon erythrostigma)

the fish will require when they grow to adulthood and reproductive maturity. It is also important to find out ahead of time where in the aquarium the preferred swimming space will be located.

Surface fishes and bottom feeders are always strongly programmed to defend their territory. Species that keep to the middle section, however, can be kept together without any problems.

Therefore, depending on the size of the aquarium, it's advisable to keep just one species each of surface fish and bottom feeders, while in the main part of the tank several tetra or barb species can happily swim together.

We want to start off by observing how the fish relate to one another, the first signs of courtship and mating, and perhaps even egg-laying in the community aquarium, before we turn to deliberate breeding attempts. There is no need to take any fish from the tank and put them into a separate aquarium. With a skilful arrangement of plants, a few young will survive even in a community aquarium, and these are often the animals that you will find the most rewarding. After all, they prove that you have planted and stocked your aquarium well.

The most important factor here is that the aquarium not be overpopulated. Three or four species with six fish each suffice fully for an aquarium of about 80 litres. If the tank is smaller, reduce the number of species even further, and instead have more fish of each kind.

When planting, the rule is there should be relatively thick vegetation growing all the way to the top, especially in the corners. This is where the fish will be likely to lay their eggs, because it is there that the young have the best protection. Well-suited to this purpose is Java moss (*Vesicularia dubyana*), a plant that can make do with little light and can also thrive in the back corners in the shadow of other plants.

The first time you are surprised to discover young fry, you will surely wonder what they have been living from before

Courting fighting fish pair (Betta splendens)

Courting combtail paradise fish (Belontia signata)

opment plan. If several males of the same species are present, competition causes them to take on their most intense colours for the first time, which was of course the original motivation for acquiring an aquarium with brilliantly coloured tropical fish. This is something you need to know when purchasing young fish. You should also know something about the kind of space

you noticed them. In fact, young fish find plenty of nutritious substances in the micro-world of an intact aquarium. These might include algae, micro organisms or mulm components—after all, they live off the same things in nature.

Live Bearers or Live-bearing Toothed Carps (Poeciliids)

There are very good reasons why live bearers are considered ideal for beginners. They don't need to stake out separate territories or swim through all parts of the aquarium and are thus considered peaceful fish. This is relative, of course, because males of the species do jockey for rank, but at least they don't kill the loser. Reproduction is the outcome of a rough process of natural selection in their home waters, for the change between rainy and dry seasons leads to strong fluctuations in the water quality. Often, only a few fish survive the dry season in the remaining isolated pools of water. When the rainy season comes again and brings better living conditions, just a few females suffice to repopulate the waters.

One thing that makes this possible is that the eggs remain in the female's body until the young have reached a certain size. Another advantage is that one mating fertilises several batches of eggs. This means that a female that has mated just once can give birth to several broods—also in an aquarium setting— without the continued presence of a male.

The ideal fish for beginners

Popular fish such as guppies (*Poecilia reticulata*), platys (*Xiphophorus maculat-*

Paradise fish pair with foam nest (Macropodus opercularis)

Albino mutants of sailfin mollies mating (Poecilia latipinna)

month. The fry are at least 5 mm long. This may still seem very small, but the young of egg-laying fish species, such as the barbs or tetras, are only 2 mm long when they hatch and only reach the size of the live-born offspring after three to four weeks. Under natural conditions, where many fry are eaten by other fish, it's quite an advantage to begin the fight for survival at a larger size.

The same applies to the aforementioned fish, the platys, swordtails and mollies, which are available for purchase in many different varieties. But if you would like to breed these fish deliberately and to ensure the survival of a maximum number of offspring, you will have to remove the pregnant female from the tank one week before the projected date of birth (on average every 28 days) and put her in a separate tank. This is no problem in the

us), swordtails (*Xiphophorus helleri*) and mollies (*Poecilia sphenops, latipinna*) bear young fairly regularly, about once a

Information

The young of live-bearing fishes, in particular, can do well in a community aquarium. Guppies are well-known for their fertility, with adult females capable of bearing up to 100 young per month. They will not all survive the perils of the community tank, but you will surely be able to take pleasure in a few new additions to your aquarium, as long as predator fish don't get carried away.

Red swordtail pair (Xiphophorus helleri)

summer, because the breeding tank does not need to be heated. But in the cooler months, this extra tank requires the same technical conditions as the main aquarium, a fact that is often forgotten.

Females about to give birth need a temperature of about 25 °C and good aeration, and one should make sure there are plenty of plants in the tank where the fry can hide right after birth. They are not yet able to swim immediately after leaving their mother's body. Their swim bladder only unfolds during the following two hours, which they spend lying quietly on a leaf. If they are disturbed, they "hop" in short spurts through the water.

These conspicuous flight movements then cause the female to pursue them and even to eat them. The only way to avoid this is to provide dense vegetation in which the young can disappear, or, as professional breeders do, a special breeding trap from which the young fish can later escape. Only with the help of this kind of set-up is it possible to determine the true number of fish in a brood.

Special breeds are more challenging

While low-maintenance varieties of fish reproduce readily, special breeding forms are much more demanding. These are descendants of species living in the wild, which stand out due to certain colour arrangements and patterns. This colouring, however, follows the rules of heredity, which the breeder has to understand well in order to maintain or improve on these special traits. This is why these fish are reserved for the true specialists.

Although a relatively small aquarium is adequate for the gravid female when she bears her young, as soon as the fish are born they will need plenty of room, special small feed, and regular water changes. So if you decide to breed fish, you will need not only a community aquarium for the breeding fish, but also small individual tanks for the gravid females and large tanks where the young

can spend their early days. Many people fail to give these requirements proper consideration. If the fry remain for too long in the small isolation tanks with their mother, the water quality there quickly worsens, affecting the quality of the growing offspring as well.

Among the live-bearing toothed carp, however, there are a few especially small species that can be kept alone in aquariums with just a few litres of water. One of these is the mosquitofish from North America (*Heterandria Formosa*). The males grow to a maximum of 2 cm, and the females get twice as big. Instead of giving birth to a large brood all at once, these fish produce one or two young per day. After about three weeks there is a slight rest period before they start producing offspring again. So if you do not have much room, but still want to enjoy the fun of raising little ones, you can have the experience with a tank of only about 5 litres capacity.

Elongate mbuna (Pseudotropheus elongatus)

Malawi golden cichlid or golden mbuna (Melano-chromis auratus), above, and Egyptian mouth-brooder (Pseudocreni-labrus multicolor), below

is protected inside the mouth of one or both parents until the fry are able to swim and escape on their own.

Of course, this biological idiosyncrasy is not the only thing that makes the mouth-brooders so interesting for us. We can't help but feel touched when we observe how a mouthbrooding mother vigilantly watches over her little ones swimming all around her, rescuing them from impending doom by gobbling them up and lovingly protecting them from harm.

For a long time, mouthbrooders were rare in the world of aquariums until, in the 1960s, several brilliantly coloured examples began to be imported from the great lakes of East Africa, and made available as pets. These new mouthbrooders capti-vate us with their colourful patterns, re-miniscent of coral reef fishes, but they only perform a limited form of mouth-brooding. Although the young are kept for several weeks in the mouth of the mother, until the yolk sac that nourishes them is used up, once they are released, they no longer return to the shelter of their mother's mouth. The fry disappear in a wink between stone crevices and only come out again when they have gained in size and self-sufficiency.

A peaceful sort: the Egyptian mouthbrooder

If you would really like to have the opportunity to observe parent fish caring for their young over a longer period, it's best to obtain one of the classic species of mouthbrooders. The first species to be imported, back in 1905 from Egypt, was the small Egyptian mouthbrooder (*Pseu-docrenilabrus multicolor*). These fish are relatively peace-loving, while the mouth-brooders from the Lakes Malawi, Tangan-yika and Victoria are larger and more colourful, but often incorrigible as well. Regardless of whether you choose the smaller or the larger species, you must always be sure to have more than one pair. The right ratio is three to five fe-males to one male.

Mouthbrooding Cichlids

In the case of the live-bearing toothed carp, we learned that the relatively large size of the fry is an advantage for them in the fight for survival. One of the most interesting brooding forms works on the same principle, the best-known members of which are the mouthbrooding cichlids. After oviposition, the entire clutch of eggs

This is due to the fact that mouthbrooder males are always ready to mate, while the females must go hungry while caring for their young in their mouths and need some time to build up strength and weight again before they can produce new eggs. If a male has only one female at his disposal, he will badger her incessantly, even if she is not ready to spawn.

The least problematic is the Egyptian mouthbrooder. Two or three males of this species and about six females can be kept in an 80-litre tank. This seems to contradict the rule of thumb we gave you at the beginning. But the fact is that only one of these males will end up ruling the aquarium, while the others have to hide. The dominant male will then display his glorious colours to scare away the others, which also makes him that much more attractive to the females. Males that have

no competition will never have to show their "true colours"!

When a female is ready to spawn, she is allowed to approach the male's territory. It might also happen that the male actively seeks her out and entices her back to his place with conspicuous courtship displays. Once there, the two circle one another and fan out a shallow hollow in the sand, which the male deepens from time to time by shovelling out sand with his mouth. After a few trial runs without laying any eggs, the female suddenly freezes, bends her back while laying some eggs in the sand, then quickly turns around and scoops them up in her mouth. The male opposite her lies on his side and presents his body. At the end of the folded anal fin is a glowing orange or reddish spot. The female swims up to the spot and tries to scoop it up as well,

Blue acara ready to spawn (Aequidens latifrons)

Mouthbrooder and young

Tip

*The aggressiveness of large mouthbrooders (*Melanochromis, Pseudotropheus *or* Labidochromis sp.*) can be much reduced when a large number of like fish are kept with other species in large aquariums. This requires high-capacity filters, because the fish eat a considerable amount of food and their excrement then rapidly contaminates the water.*

*Convict cichlid (*Cichlasoma nigrofasciatum)

since it is the same colour as the eggs she has just laid. This is how the sperm cells produced by the male join the eggs in the mother's mouth. This is where fertilisation takes place. Within just an hour, a well-nourished, 10 cm-long female can lay up to 100 eggs and have them fertilised in this manner. When she's finished, her body will be perceptibly thinner, but her mouth with its flexible throat skin will be conspicuously swollen. From this point on, the female no longer reacts to the male's courtship displays and has to hide, as the male only allows females in his territory that are ready to spawn.

Caution is advisable

Careful breeders now remove the female from the aquarium. This can work out well if it is possible to accomplish the move without disrupting her too much. But when they are caught in a net, the females tend to spit out their fry and not take them up again. Moving the female is therefore best done at night, using a torch to determine her location and catching her up by surprise in a large enough container so that she doesn't take much notice.

In the smaller mouthbrooder species it takes about 14 days for the eggs to develop, depending on the temperature, and the large varieties might require three to four weeks. The thin skin of the throat and the frequently gaping mouth allow you to follow the development of the young. The large yolk sacs slowly grow smaller, soon the eyes can be seen, and just before releasing her young the female swims to the bottom of the tank and becomes increasingly shy. When you see the fry for the first time, that doesn't necessarily mean that this is their first time out. But by the first time you observe them, at the latest, you have to make sure to provide the young and their mother with appropriate food. Just to be sure, you can also do this a few days earlier. The danger of the young being eaten by the mother is nonexistant for this species. Instead, it has been observed that the female sometimes lays the eggs or larvae down for a few minutes to eat and then gathers them up again.

Especially in the case of the small mouthbrooder, it is now fun to watch how the mother continues for several days to snap up her young every time danger lurks, and then spit them out again and, in particular in the evening, how she waves her fins to entice her young to come back into the safety of her mouth. These phases are missing in the large mouthbrooders, which are however kept more frequently these days due to their bright colours. The fry, which measure almost 1 cm, are easy to raise since they eagerly snap up any food they can handle.

Many mouthbrooders are aggressive

Understandably, the aquarium owner tends to pay a great deal of attention to the young fry and neglect their mother. But it is a mistake to place the physically weakened female right back in with the male. She should first be given a chance to regenerate her strength for a while, surrounded by her brood. Inexperienced aquarium owners often complain that

only the males of their mouthbrooders survive, while the females tend to die early. This is solely attributable to the fact that the exhausted females are returned to the community tank too early and are thus vulnerable to the males' attacks. These are not the right conditions for living to a ripe old age!

Other Cichlids

The mouthbrooders described in the previous sections personify a special method for caring for their young developed by the cichlids, a variety of fish that is beloved by aquarium fans, and not only for their beautiful colours. All cichlid species are especially protective of their spawn and young.

Of course, their intensive child-rearing takes place within a hard-fought territory that they must continue to defend, giving them a reputation for being "com-

bative", "snappish" and "incompatible". But these are appraisals that stem from false expectations on the part of aquarium owners. Those who find cichlids beautiful and who care for them according to their needs usually do not need to

Schwartz's catfish (Corydoras schwartzi)

Venezuelan ram cichlid with young (Mikrogeophagus ramirezi)

worry about them remaining healthy and living out their lives. However, it must be remembered that these lives also include reaching reproductive maturity and showing the typical behaviour connected with the reproductive process.

You can't prevent this! And no one would really want to. After all, it's one of the most wonderful experiences you can have with your aquarium, a young pair swimming alongside their growing brood. The fact that this forces other fish to play the role of enemies or scapegoats is likewise just a part of nature. The only thing to do is to choose other fish that are either able to escape the attacks of the parents, or which keep to spaces where they are safe from assault, for example the surface of the tank.

Which of the over 100 species of cichlid available you decide to keep depends in part on the size of your aquarium. They all need quite a lot of space, even if the designation of some of them as dwarf cichlids might give the impression that they can be kept in extremely small quarters. Dwarf cichlids are not a true systematically defined zoological group. The term is used instead to refer to species in which the males grow no larger than 10–12 cm. These small varieties tend to make up for what they lack in size with an especially large dose of aggressiveness, and so the dwarf cichlids, in particular the females, can be quite cantankerous when it comes to protecting their young.

When you buy young cichlids at the store, you will find yourself waiting in anxious anticipation to figure out what gender they are. It is advisable to purchase eight to ten young fish, although you might be lucky enough to get a pair when you buy just six. Patience is of the essence—it may take almost a year with smaller species, and up to three years with larger ones, before you know for sure what you have in your tank. The young fish at first live together in absolute harmony. A tussle now and then is normal, even among peaceful fish like the swordtails.

Not until the fish are just about to reach reproductive maturity do the battles become more determined. The future males defend their territory and weaker fish have to submit. The same kind of confrontations can take place among females, and the strongest of them will in turn be examined by the dominant male as a potential partner.

Sometimes, but not as a rule, this strong female will be accepted as partner. From this point on it is better to remove the other fish of the same species from the aquarium, since the new couple will ruthlessly drive all the others off their territory during the time leading up to spawning. For some of the less tolerant breeds this territory might indeed encompass the entire aquarium! So cichlids are not necessarily suitable for every community tank.

*Altum angelfish
(Pterophyllum altum)*

Young angelfish

Mouthbrooder holding young in its mouth

Nanochromis parilus

The angelfish is also a cichlid

One of the most well-known of the cichlids is the angelfish (*Pterophyllum scalare*). It should not be kept among other fish in a community aquarium. It is better to give them a whole aquarium as their undisputed realm, and to add a few complementary species. The surface might be occupied by a few tetras of the *Nannostomus* genus, while a few armoured catfish (*Corydoras genus*) on the bottom won't bother anyone, and live-bearing toothed carp (*Poeciliidae*) will be easily driven away as necessary.

The fry of the latter varieties of fish represent a welcome food supplement and these species, for example swordtails, are thus often kept deliberately with the angelfish in breeding aquariums. Within a year of purchase, the gender of the angelfish is easy to determine, even if the literature is not always in agreement on this point. Males are always bigger and have a wide concave forehead, while the upper head line of the female remains almost straight.

Show-offs and show-downs in the aquarium

Even the quite placid angelfish go through a "tough guy" phase when they're young—the males, lying atilt in the water, go at one another and try to impress the others with their prowess. They might even lock jaws or shove each other roughly. Here as well, their goal is to carve out a territory in which one male is the absolute ruler. Soon, one of the females will join him and they will begin together to clean a long leaf growing at a slant or straight upward. If the right kind of plant is lacking, angelfish will also attach their eggs to heaters, pipes or the aquarium walls.

Spawning angelfish

Although many claim that pairs that have chosen one another will also take good care of their young, this is not always true. There are already signs at the first spawning whether the pair is a good match or not. As a rule, the closer together the eggs are and the more self-contained the clump looks, the more harmonious the pair. But if the eggs are laid out in irregular strips and distributed over the whole leaf, either the pair is too young and still needs some practice, or they are simply incompatible. The breeder should then intervene and pair up the male in his territory with another female. Often, it is necessary to try out several females before a good pairing combination is found.

Professionals count on profit

This is where the hobby breeder and the professional part ways. The pro is only interested in the spawn. He removes the

leaf from the tank and raises the young without the parents' care. Pairs who lose their brood in this way might lay new eggs in as little as ten to 14 days, depending on how well they are fed. This is what a professional breeding operation depends on. But the hobbyist is more interested in watching the parents look after their young. The greater the number of fry, from which later breeding pairs can be raised, the greater the probability of mates being found that fit together well and later care well for their young. Artificial breeding has not by any means led to the fish losing the ability to raise their own young. Even in nature, not all pairs are equally good parents, and natural selection sees to it that the young of more caring parents have a better chance of survival. In our fast-paced times, even aquarium owners have become less patient and sometimes simply give up too early when a young pair does not harmonise well the first time they spawn.

Males and females care for their young

In the best-case scenario, the male guards the space around the plant where the eggs have been laid, while the female looks after the eggs. By constantly dabbing at them with her mouth, she removes any films covering the leaf, destroys unfertilised eggs, and energetically waves her breast fins to increase water circulation. Depending on the water temperature, which must not fall below 25 °C, the young fish hatch any time from three to five days after egg-laying. At first it looks as if the eggs have grown tails. Both parents take the fry in their mouths and spit them out again in a little clump. Once again, the temperature determines when the young attempt to swim for the first time. Some early bloomers are caught up again by their parents, who don't eat them but spit them out again in a small clump. Finally, the little ones set out in a school away from their parents, still swimming a little awkwardly. They don't look like

angelfish yet, but rather like young cichlids: they have a steep forehead and round, clumsy body with a frantically waving little tail. Now is high time to make sure they get food that's right for their size. A good choice is *nauplii*—the freshly hatched larvae of brine shrimp (*Artemia salina*). These are available at pet shops in the form of hard-shelled eggs, which can be hatched at home in well-aerated saline water. In their first hours the larvae are still soft and can easily be sucked up by the young fish. After just one day, their shell already becomes hard and the fry will have difficulties swallowing them. This means that during the first week a fresh batch of brine shrimp has to be hatched each day for the daily feeding.

In a community aquarium with appropriate complementary fishes, a good breeding pair will see to it that no enemies harm their young. You can support their care efforts by keeping a weak light on even at night during the first week, for example a desk lamp at some distance from

Cockatoo cichlid male (Apistogramma cacatuoides)

101

the aquarium. Very few aquarium lights are equipped with a dimmer, so the young might be startled when the lights suddenly go out and begin to swim around the tank. This may break up the school and the parents quickly lose control over the situation.

The young grow and change

Pearl gourami pair spawning (Trichogaster leeri)

At the end of the second week, the body form of the young fish begins to change. The back is now higher and the extended

dorsal and anal fins begin to appear. This is the phase that even experienced aquarium owners find particularly enchanting: the elegantly gliding older fish with the clumsy young ones darting along beside them.

What has been described here based on the example of angelfish in principle holds true for all cichlids: you should let pairs of young fish get together on their own, give them plenty of places where they can spawn and, especially through the presence of other fish, help trigger their instincts to care for their young and defend their territory. The cichlids are divided into two different groups according to how they lay their eggs: open and shelter brooders. The boundaries between them are fluid, although there are typical representatives of each category. You might also get to know certain pairs that always hide their eggs, even though they belong to a species of open brooders.

However, all dwarf cichlids of the *Apistogramma* genus consistently lay their eggs in caves or rock crevices and never in the open on an easily visible surface.

Finally, in order not to leave anything out, there is even a grey area between the open brooders and mouthbrooders. This is occupied by the species that at first spawn like open brooders, but later take the eggs or larvae into their mouth and keep them there until the fry are able to swim on their own.

All in all, the cichlids, many varieties of which come from South America and Africa, but which can also be found in Madagascar and the Indian Peninsula, provide the aquarium owner with a wide choice of variations in brooding habits. It's easy to understand why these brilliantly coloured and reproductively fascinating species have so many fans.

Labyrinth Fish or Anabantids

Up until now we have proceeded in the order of the easiest-to-raise young fish to those that are more difficult. The larger the young fry are when they start their lives, the less work the breeder has in offering them appropriate food and pulling them through to adulthood.

The labyrinth fishes we will now describe are a group that is just as colourful as the cichlids and that exhibits brooding behaviour that is every bit as interesting. Raising the young is much more difficult, however, because they are extremely small in comparison.

In nature there are two principles by which a species ensures its preservation through its offspring: either a huge number of young are produced, of which at least a few will grow up and attain reproductive maturity; or the number of offspring is limited, but protected by a focus on brood care. Living births, mouth brooding and brood care have been typical of the fish groups we have looked at thus far, all of whom give birth to relatively large young.

The males are in charge of the brood

Brood care among the labyrinth fishes is the province of one gender only—the males. They carve out a territory, build a foam nest out of myriad air bubbles enveloped in saliva (in which the eggs are embedded) watch over this nest and the eggs, and even look out for the hatched young for a few days. Often, the eggs from several females are gathered together in one such a nest. Well-developed females, for example those of the three-spot gourami (*Trichogaster trichopterus*) species and their breeding forms, can lay some 1,000 eggs.

This challenges the breeder to provide enough first food for the tiny fry. But they are not big enough to handle the easy-to-obtain brine shrimp nauplii until after about seven to ten days. *Infusoria* such as *Rotifera* or the larvae of domestic Cyclops, on the other hand, are only available in adequate quantities during certain seasons—at least in most climes—which does make

breeding labyrinth fish, and especially raising their young, quite a challenging undertaking.

By contrast, getting these fish to spawn is quite easy. This happens virtually on its own in community aquariums of adequate size, accompanied however—for those fish who care for their brood—by the usual territorial fights and chasing away of intruders, which may be harmed and even killed in the process. This can happen among the colourful labyrinth fish just as it does with the cichlids.

The paradise fish is "out of fashion"

Despite its gorgeous colours and interesting brood care, the oldest aquarium pet, the paradise fish (*Macropodus opercularis*), is no longer anywhere near as popular as in the early days of the hobby.

By contrast, the various breeding forms of the gourami can be found today in many community aquariums: blue, silver, gold and marbled. They are introduced into

Pearl gourami at its foam nest

Paradise fish pair spawning (Macropodus opercularis)

only is the female forced to hide from that point on—every other fish in the tank is chased relentlessly, as well. You are well advised not to purchase this widely available fish without first taking into consideration the possible later consequences.

Small gouramis are easier to keep

Easier to handle, but not entirely without risk, are the smaller gouramis of the *Colisa* genus. These include the dwarf gourami (*Colisa lalia*), which is available in several breeding forms, and the thick-lipped gourami (*Colisa labiosa*). In particular the original form of the former species is one of the most beautiful aquarium fish, since at 5 cm it grows to a considerable length even for medium-sized aquariums. These animals become hard to deal with only during mating season. It is then better to keep several pairs by themselves in a large aquarium than to keep one alone in a community aquarium. Several males will keep each other busy with constant tussles, but at least they then leave the other fish in peace. A single male, on the other hand, is able to zero in on every single "enemy". Here, too, the female will be just another potential victim once she has laid her eggs. Raising the young is just as difficult as with the large *Trichogaster* genus, or just as easy if you have the right food available in adequate quantities.

Fighting fish with foam nest (Betta splendens)

the aquarium as young fish without hesitation and seem to create few problems for their fans—at least I have not heard many complaints. Many years of active experience in breeding these fish, however, has proven that fully-grown males are capable of tyrannising even large aquariums once a foam nest has been built or eggs have been laid there. Not

Thick-lipped gouramis mating (Colisa labiosa)

Fighting fish males battle to the blood

At the extreme end of the scale when it comes to territorial defence are the aptly named Siamese fighting fish or bettas (*Betta splendens*). In fact, it is really only possible to have one male per aquarium and, often enough, one hears complaints from betta-lovers that this one fish has harmed other aquarium inhabitants. There is only one solution in this case, which reminds one of the recommendations made for mouthbrooders, and that is to keep several females for one male. If just a single pair lives in the aquarium, the female will wind up completely over-worked and almost always on the lam. With several females reaching maturity at different times, however, the male will have plenty to keep him busy and won't have time to focus on one hapless vic-tim. Raising the young fighting fish, pro-vided you have the right food on hand for the little ones, is perhaps the easiest part. It is made more difficult, however, by the fact that you will have to isolate each male after it reaches about 3 cm in length, and bring it up alone. When they reach this size they start to fight amongst themselves and damage each other's fins.

Fewer young, but larger in size

While the species cited above produce large quantities of fry, there are also some breeds of labyrinth fish that lay only a small number of eggs and ensure their survival through mouthbrooding. Once hatched, the young fish are several times the size of the fry produced in large masses, giving them a substantial survival advantage under natural condi-tions. With the exception of the very at-tractive chocolate gouramis of the genus *Sphaerichthys*, most of the common mouthbrooding labyrinth fish are quite unspectacular-looking and are thus only found among specialists.

Rainbow Fish or Melanotaenids

It is not only in nature that species lay-ing numerous eggs have a better chance of seeing some young fish grow to mat-urity—this strategy works to their benefit in the aquarium as well. When these egg masses are not laid all at the same time, but rather in portions over the course of several days, the fish are referred to as repeat spawners. Among them are some brilliantly coloured species that first cap-tured attention just two decades ago.

Chocolate gouramis (Sphaerichthys osphromenoides)

Boeseman's rainbowfish (Melanotaenia boesemani)

Cherry barb
(Barbus titteya)

crossbreeds yields fish that are as attractive as the original breeds. Therefore, breeders now follow the rule of keeping only one species per aquarium in order to prevent random bastardisations. Of course, one cannot tell hobbyists what to do, but we can at least make a recommendation for what's best. The disappointment will be great if the aquarium owner goes to a lot of effort to pull through just a few tiny young fish to maturity, only to find out that they are the unattractive products of accidental interbreeding.

Rainbow fish have proven ideal for a special form of aquarium—there are hobbyists who collect aquatic plants from all over the world and find pleasure in achieving highly decorative arrangements of this greenery. If a single species of rainbow fish is kept in this type of aquarium, they are virtually guaranteed never to die out. Eggs will be laid continually, with fry being hatched every day, and the growing fish will supplement the school as the older ones die out. One might object that this would lead to a larger population than the aquarium can comfortably hold. But this will hardly be the case because, of all the young fish born, only a few will come through to maturity. The older youngsters keep the following generations in check by feeding on them, while the mature fish don't bother the younger ones. With this kind of fish as well, there are larger, medium and smaller varieties, which in principle all have similar requirements and can live in the surface area of any community aquarium. The larger breeds include the red rainbowfish (*Glossolepis incisus*). These are a stunning red colour when full-grown and their head form is reminiscent of that of mature salmon. However, this species is not the best one for impatient aquarium fans, as the young stay silver-grey for almost a year before attaining maturity and their rich red colour.

The medium-sized varieties include Macculloch's rainbowfish (*Melanotaenia macculochi*), which has been an aquarium

As with all mass producers, the young fish of these species are also very small and difficult to raise. And another limitation must be considered as well in the case of the rainbow fish. All of these species are geologically quite young and tend to interbreed in the aquarium environment. By now, deliberate breeding experiments have revealed that none of the possible

pet for over 50 years. Due to selective breeding, the fish available on the market vary strongly in quality. All fin edges should be an intensive red—unfortunately, dealers do not always check for this quality attribute.

It is more difficult to obtain the attractive small species. They can usually be purchased only from specialists and rarely make their way into pet stores. These include not only the *Pseudomugil* species (formerly classified in part under the *Popondetta* genus), but also the attractive blue *Melanotaenia praecox*, commonly known as the dwarf or neon rainbowfish. But these are the kind of special fish you should perhaps save for a later time, once you have gotten to know some other species well and have bred them successfully.

In addition to the rotifera and cyclops larvae already mentioned as a food source for tiny young labyrinth fish, at least a few rainbow fish fry will survive their first days and weeks if you break up the feed flakes into a fine powder for them before scattering them on the water. This is just right for their habit of living close to the surface, and often you will be amazed that you didn't even notice the young fish who have been living off the food they have found in the aquarium. But this can only happen if, besides the parents, there are no other fish sharing the tank with them.

Barbs and Rasboras (Cyprinids)

The great majority of barbs and rasboras available today in stores come from overseas breeding farms and not from European sources. Even fish-lovers tend to prefer the low-maintenance cichlids or live-bearers to the barbs and rasboras, which often bear quite minuscule young. These fish were traditionally bred in specially equipped small tanks without any gravel or sand on the bottom. Instead, an egg mesh would be installed at the

bottom of the tank, because almost all species chase after their spawn after egg-laying and consume it. After spawning, the parents must thus be removed from the tank and the fry, which can swim after five days, must be raised on rotifera

White cloud mountain minnow (Tanichthys albonubes)

Ticto barb (Barbus ticto)

organisms to get them through their first days. They only become noticeable once they develop an unmistakable glowing blue stripe that reminds one of young neon tetras. By that time, they are already past the rough times and can easily be raised on finely pulverised flake food. For these fish, too, the older juveniles are more dangerous than the parents, so that the population will never get out of hand. If you want more survivors, you can simply remove the more mature amongst the younger fish and raise them in a separate tank.

Harlequin rasboras for the advanced beginner

For a long time, the coveted but difficult-to-raise harlequin rasbora (*Rasbora heteromorpha*) represented a special case. Over 60 years ago, when the neon tetra had just been discovered, breeding fish only succeeded in extremely soft and acidic water. This can be achieved today with little effort, which means that breeding the harlequin rasbora is no longer a real challenge. Strangely enough though, this species' reputation among aquarium owners as a problem fish has not managed to catch up with reality. Even distinguishing males from females is quite straightforward: in males the black wedge shape extends further down the stomach, coming to a point, while in females there is a light-coloured zone several millimetres wide between the lower edge of the black marking and the line of the stomach.

That does not yet ensure that every male will spawn with every female. An elaborate mating game, during which the male swims above the female's back, trying to test whether synchronicity of movement can be achieved, is the first step in the process. Then the female hides herself under a leaf, turning onto her back with her belly pointing upward, while the male loops himself around her back like a horseshoe. During this embrace the eggs are attached to the

or cyclops larvae. Hardly anyone bothers to go to this trouble anymore, although the amount of effort required, with the exception of the special feed, is not as great as it is usually presented.

A particularly easy breed

On another note, I'd like to introduce you to one fish that, like the rainbow fish, can be kept in a single-species aquarium and will reproduce effortlessly. This is the White Cloud Mountain minnow (*Tanichthys albonubes*). A troop of ten to 15 fish will be bound to include enough males and females for breeding. These can be raised easily and kept healthy with a good flaked food and occasional frozen food treats. Since they are also repeat spawners, they will lay eggs nearly every day. The tiny fry will be ignored by the parents and are at first hard for the inexperienced fish-fan to identify. They keep to the water's surface and evidently find there—and in the feathery water plants like Java moss and milfoil (*Myriophyllum*)—enough micro

bottom side of the leaf. According to my own observations, only those eggs that do not stick and thus fall to the ground are consumed.

The fry that hatch in 36 hours attach themselves to the tank's walls or between the plants and are first seen swimming in open water after five days. They are amazingly large and long, although not as large as the young mouthbrooders. Their relatively big mouth allows them to start eating brine shrimp nauplii immediately, so that raising them is even quite an easy proposition. In sum, there is really no good reason why aquarium owners should be hesitant to raise harlequin rasboras for themselves.

Tetras (Characins)

The sweeping judgment usually made about this very multifaceted and varied fish group is as oversimplified as it is unfounded: they are dismissed as school fish, which can only be bred in soft water with a lot of work, but are fine as inhabitants of a community tank. There are whole books on the subject of tetras alone, but these are still inadequate at describing the wide variety of forms and living habits of the South American and African fishes that are all grouped together under the name tetra. It is equally difficult to provide basic information here about raising all kinds of tetras, since there are so few rules that apply to all.

*Neon tetras thrive
in soft, acidic water*

It is true that a breeder must provide soft and acidic water if he or she wishes to raise the popular neon tetras (*Paracheirodon innesi*), and that the fry require a great deal of loving care during the first few weeks. The least little bit of bacterial water contamination can lead to the loss of the whole brood.

But nobody starts with the most difficult fish first! For the first breeding attempts

Flame tetras (Hyphessobrycon flammeus)

it makes sense to choose an easy-to-breed species such as the flame tetra (*Hyphessobrycon flammeus*), whose young will also hatch in somewhat harder water and can be fed in their early days with finely ground flakes until they can handle brine shrimp nauplii. For this variety, the traditional breeding method also consisted for a long time of a glass tank fitted with an egg mesh instead of sand, into which one or more pairs would be put to spawn. From the multitude of eggs, enough young fish would survive to make breeding successful even for beginners.

*Tetras who look after
their brood are the exception*

Even among the tetras there are a few species that care for their brood, in the genera *Copella* and *Pyrrhulina*. One of these, the splashing tetra (*Copella arnoldi*), is remarkable for its very peculiar re-

109

propriately. There must be 6–10 cm of air space between the water and the tank lid. You can arrange the leaves of a pothos or philodendron plant in this space, fixing them to the side of the tank. A more primitive method consists in laying a piece of cardboard on the lid. Male splashing tetras immediately respond to this invitation and station themselves underneath the leaves or cardboard. After a few agitated swimming phases, they take on a vertical position and jump under the leaves or attach themselves to the lid. Once they have gotten a feeling for the distance required, they take the spawning-ready female with them on their next jump, and the eggs are attached outside the water. After each spawning, the fish fall back into the water and jump out again. Especially energetic males can accumulate gigantic collections of more than 100 eggs with several females. Afterwards, the male remains stationed under the eggs and splashes them with water from time to time until the young hatch and fall into the aquarium with the water droplets.

Along with raising young angelfish, observing this unique behaviour, which is found nowhere else in the fish world, is a definite highlight for the aquarium fan. But it also demonstrates that "the tetras" cannot really be treated indiscriminately. The related *Pyrrhulina* species lay eggs on a leaf, and the male remains close by to guard them. One might think he has

Ornate tetras

Red neon or cardinal tetras

productive method. The males occupy territories at the surface of the aquarium, which unquestionably must be set up ap-

consumed the young after they hatch, but after 14 days there they are, having grown up invisibly somewhere in the tank.

There's a reason for delayed spawning

Other tetras mate without at first laying any eggs. The females store the sperm and wait until living conditions are right and food is available in plenty before forming eggs, which they then lay without needing a male's assistance. The species that follow this strategy include the swordtail characin (*Corynopoma riisei*) and some gorgeous glowing blue tetras of the genus *Mimagoniates*.

Among the tetras, there are those who lay their eggs high up and those who dig hollows in the ground and look after their young, like the cichlids do. All in all, we are nowhere near to having catalogued all the multifarious forms of behaviour found in the many varieties of tetra. It should be pointed out, however, that most of our observations have been made in the aquarium and were only later confirmed by studies carried out under natural conditions.

A Final Word...

At the beginning of the science of aquariums, the aim was just to keep single fish obtained from exotic waters alive under artificial conditions. We slowly saw which temperatures they prefer, tried out different kinds of feed, and considered ourselves successful if the animals were still alive after one year.

It took some time before we learned to distinguish between the genders of each species. Science was not always helpful. Often, in the case of males and females that develop quite differently, they would be registered as two different species. Day-to-day aquarium practice helped, in terms of naming as well, to classify together the fish that belonged together. Once an aquarium owner had a pair in the tank and cared for them properly, it was not long before they would form and lay eggs. Their normal life cycle began to take place in the aquarium environment.

This was most successful with fish that are used to dealing with fluctuating conditions in their natural habitats: the live bearers. Their ability to give birth to live young caused quite a sensation when they were discovered. These were the fish that helped aquariums attain the popularity they still enjoy today, even though other, more colourful varieties had already been available for decades. Later groups of fish

Marbled hatchetfish (Carnegiella strigata strigata)

Bumblebee goby from Southeast Asia

Steel-blue killifish (Aphyosemion gardneri)

would place higher demands on care, food and breeding. For a long time there was no precise and usable knowledge available on water chemistry, so it was up to aquarium owners to experiment. In spite of many missteps along the way, they eventually achieved positive results. Since water composition differs from re-

gion to region, it was only realised gradually that soft water could form an advantage in fish breeding. In Germany, areas with soft water are in the low mountain rages, chiefly in Saxony, Thuringia and the Harz, and so this is where the first professional breeding farms were established. The breeders working there were forced to maintain optimal conditions to ensure maximum production, while hobbyists were free to experiment, trying to determine what conditions were best for the new imports. In this way the most successful hobby breeders went on to become the next generation of professional breeders.

This development continued until about mid-century. By then it was less expensive for retail shops to import cheaper fish from overseas farms. In tropical countries there is no need to pay the high heating costs required in Europe, wages are much lower and, even with the cost of air transport figured in, aquarium fish from foreign farms are still more reasonable than those raised in Europe. As a result, the breeding of aquarium fish in Europe has steadily dwindled, with just a few breeders able to remain competitive. What's left are experiment-happy aquarium owners.

Every year, uncharted territories continue to be explored and new fish species discovered. Presently, there is quite a lot of interest in various catfish-type species. Modern filtration technology has made it possible to keep very high-maintenance fish, which are used to a strong current, in the modern aquarium. And once we know the secret to keeping them healthy, it is not long before they begin to reproduce in captivity. If a pair manages to do this spontaneously, the owner has a basis on which to develop a method for predictable breeding results.

But in order to be able to handle such precious occurrences with the requisite sure instincts, the breeder has to have finely honed skills at his disposal. These are gained through day-to-day practice, and must be cultivated and maintained.

This is lacking a bit these days, because it's so easy just to go the fish store and pick out a few fish from the huge selection available for every possible taste. Once the first fish have lived out their lives, you can just go and buy some new ones. It used to be that aquarium owners were forced to keep up their stock by doing their own breeding and to share the results with others. That kept them fit in breeding knowledge and skills, and new acquisitions were a rare highlight.

The current efforts to preserve animal species from extinction, along with legislation designed to protect the environment, will have an influence on today's aquarium fish market. The time may be drawing near when the only fish allowed to be sold in shops will be those raised in the immediate vicinity. The significance of aquarium-keeping also lies in creating a bridge between the traditional and future breeding culture, by forming associations and organisations that can speak with a united voice and which can preserve the knowledge that we have acquired so far.

*Cuban limias
(Limia vittata)*

*Swordtail characin
(Corynopoma riisei)*

Even Fish Can
Get Sick Sometimes

Fish are unfortunately not immune to diseases. These can be caused by parasites, viruses, bacteria, overfeeding, stress, toxins in the water and other factors. Often the beginner has a difficult time recognising a sickness in time and undertaking the necessary treatment. Although there are a wide range of effective medications available today, before you resort to them (in effect putting "poison" in the water), you should know exactly which disease your fish are suffering from. If you know or have the feeling that one or more of your fish are ill, you should remove them as quickly as possible from the common aquarium and put them into

*Pumpkinseed sunfish (*Lepomis gibbosus*)*

a separate quarantine tank with a slightly elevated water temperature. Some diseases exhibit visible symptoms such as a white film or spots on the fish's scales; or you might observe the fish trying to scratch itself on roots or rocks. This could be a sign of a parasitic or fungal infection, which can be treated with a liquid broad-spectrum medication. A fish might also exhibit signs of malnutrition caused by feed that is not appropriate to its species. A varied diet including various kinds of feed usually prevents this problem. Sometimes fish suddenly grow pale and become quite unsightly. They are perhaps lacking a certain ingredient in their feed that is responsible for pigmentation. A reputable dealer will know which species need special food

*Black ruby barb (*Barbus nigrofasciatus*)*

supplements in order to regain the glowing colours of good health. Growth disturbances also indicate poor or inappropriate nutrition. However, by the time these are noticeable, they are difficult to correct. If the fish in your aquarium are acting unusually agitated, abruptly darting to and fro, or if they try to jump out of the tank or come to the surface gasping for air, it could be that a toxin has made its way into the water, or that overpopulation of the tank or poor filter performance has led to a dangerous accumulation of nitrites or ammoniac. You can still remedy the situation, as long as you haven't waited too

long, by changing part of the water or installing a stronger filter. If symptoms appear with which you are unfamiliar—and there are plenty of possibilities—you can

try to ask for advice from a fish dealer, from the fish-tender at a public aquarium, or from an experienced ornamental fish owner. It's usually not possible to cure fish once they are seriously ill—but you can in any event shorten their suffering.

Opposite page: Chocolate oranda goldfish

Red and white ryukin

Information

One widespread fish disease is dropsy, or ascites. This is caused by bacteria and eventually destroys the liver. When bodily fluids get into the abdominal cavity, the fish looks bloated and the scales seem raised. This is a condition that is nearly impossible to cure. The affected fish must be removed from the tank as quickly as possible.

View of a community aquarium

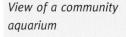

Coldwater Fish
Living in Fresh Water

Information

As soon as you start looking for literature on coldwater fish and dealers that sell them, you will be surprised to learn that there is not much available on the market. It's easiest to find information on caring for and breeding prized domestic fish such as the trout, grayling, pike or walleye. But these are the species that are the most demanding in terms of water quality and oxygen supply, and therefore cannot be recommended with good conscience to the beginner.

Fish biotope: a small European lake

When aquarium owners and avid fish fans speak about ornamental fishes, they almost always mean fish found in the tropics. About five dozen different species form the central core of warmwater aquarium fish.

Nevertheless, there are also people who are interested in devoting their attention to domestic fishes or other species that live in cooler waters. Since there is little information available in this area, it's best to obtain the technical equipment and detailed knowledge you need not from books, but from a professional fish-breeding facility. But you will soon find out that the fish there are not kept in tanks, but in large ponds and breeding pools instead.

If you're interested in trying out a few less demanding coldwater fish and your choice does not depend on looks alone, but you're ready to give some less spectacular-looking breeds a chance, then the following will provide you with a few important tips and guidelines. To save space, we have gathered the information together as a general overview—with the exception of the goldfish and kois, which we will treat in greater detail. However, this general information should still be sufficient as a basis upon which to reach your decision, and to show you that not only colourful, tropical species can make for an exciting hobby.

Goldfish (Carassius auratus auratus)

Through the years a number of different goldfish colour mutations have emerged—100 are known today—and a variety of breeding forms. The gibel carp evidently has a natural tendency to form different-coloured variants.

The oldest red and red-and-white-checked forms appeared in fifth-century China. The first goldfish arrived in Japan around 1500 and they had their heyday there during the following two centuries. From Japan and China, these prized fish, which at that time were worth their weight in gold, made their way to other Asian countries. Sometime at the end of the seventeenth and beginning of the eighteenth century, the first goldfishes came to Europe, landing initially in Great Britain. Whether they were bred there first, or in Holland as other sources allege, is ultimately of little interest to the goldfish fan. What is important is that the beautiful fish took Europe by storm during the second half of the eighteenth century.

For a long time goldfish were the most popular aquarium fish. They were kept in round "goldfish bowls", in which the non-demanding and adaptable animals could live out an uneventful life.

When the aquarium industry began to manufacture small heating elements and filters, however, tropical fish gradually captured the public's interest, replacing the goldfish to some extent as the highlight in many living rooms. However, the goldfish still maintains a certain amount of popularity today, especially in garden ponds and larger indoor aquariums. Indeed, it appears as if this breed is in the process today of gaining more and more fans.

New and often quite spectacular breeds reach our shores regularly from China, Japan and the Far East. These are at first

sold for exorbitant prices—several thousand pounds per fish is not unheard of—but frequently disappear from the scene after just a few years.

The beginner, at least, should opt instead for the plain breeding forms rather than those with notoriously peculiar features such as veiltails, telescope eyes or celestial eyes, which are sometimes quite pathetic creatures.

The gibel carp is not much of a looker

The wild form of the goldfish, the gibel carp, also known as the Prussian, German or silver crucian carp, reaches a length of 20–25 cm, and sometimes even 40 cm. It looks like a standard carp, but is a little slimmer. The base colour is a silvery greyish blue with darker pigmentation on belly and back. Reddish and silvery mutations also exist. The domesticated form of the Chinese gibel carp, the goldfish, grows to somewhere between 10 and 30 cm long, depending on the aquarium or garden pond. The smaller the area they inhabit, the smaller the fish remain. The body of the plain goldfish is long and slim with quite a high back and well-defined fins. However, there are breeds with features such as celestial, telescope or bubble eyes, or veiltails that look quite different from the conventional goldfish. The basic colours were originally red, reddish gold and silver. But in the course of time other colour variations were bred, including white, brown, red and white, blue with dark spots and others. Some might seem hard to tell apart from Japanese kois, but the latter are actually easily identified by their whiskers, or barbels.

Males and females look almost alike

Except for during mating time, it is hard to tell male goldfish apart from females. The males are somewhat slimmer, but you'll need some experience before you can recognise this subtle difference! Another distinguishing feature is the form of the anal region. In adult males two to three years old it is slightly recessed, while in mature females it is slightly convex and pointed. One sure way to tell them apart is the spawning rash that fertile males display on their gill covers and pectoral fins at mating time. If you have several fish in a garden pond or aquarium, you can tell the genders apart at mating time by their behaviour as well.

If you would like to breed your goldfish, it is advisable to consult a breeder or experienced goldfish-owner to help you identify the gender of the fish you have. Otherwise, reproduction will more or less be left up to chance. That would be a shame, because deliberate breeding is not particularly difficult and the development of the young brood is fascinating for the whole family.

Ryukin

Information
The goldfish is a breeding form that was created from wild gibel carp, a species living throughout Europe. Their ancestor in turn was the Chinese subspecies Carassius a. auratus. The gibel carp was domesticated in China more than 1,500 years ago. Goldfish were later released into lakes and other standing waters all over the world and, without human assistance (feeding, controlled temperatures) eventually adapted to these natural conditions.

Gibel carp (Carassius auratus gibelio)—the wild form of the goldfish

Sarasa comet

Steel blue oranda

Good-bye goldfish bowl, hello spacious aquarium

The days of goldfish bowls should once and for all be relegated to the past. First of all, they are much too small. Secondly, because of the small opening at the top the water contains far too little oxygen, forcing the animals to swim to the surface at regular intervals and "gasp for air". Thirdly, since there is no filter and excrement will quickly accumulate, the water has to be changed every single day. This is a stressful ordeal for the fish and also goes against the Animal Protection Act, which states that every animal "must be fed, cared for and kept in a way consistent with its behaviour".

A tank with a side length of 90–100 cm and a corresponding height and width (approx. 50 x 50 cm) is recommended for goldfish. This size tank will hold about 200–250 litres of water. If we assume that each fish needs about three litres per centimetre, this means you can keep 70–80 cm of total fish length in your aquarium. When buying fish sized 4–6 cm, however, keep in mind that they will grow quite large when housed in a 200-litre aquarium, up to 15–20 cm. When applying the litre/centimetre equation, therefore, it should be based on full-grown fish instead of the young ones you will be purchasing. In other words, the above-cited 70–80 cm of fish only allow for four, or at the most six, fish! If you try to keep more fish, the tank will become overpopulated and it will be difficult to achieve an equilibrium between plants, fish and a healthy nitrogen cycle.

No special knowledge or skills required: the goldfish aquarium

Setting up a goldfish pond or tank is simple and requires little technical effort. The tank bed consists of pebbles that have been washed several times, sized 4–6 mm. The bed should be about 10 mm deeper in front and deepest in one of the front corners. Food remains, mulm and dead plant debris will tend to settle in this corner and are then easy to vacuum right up. You should be cautious in choosing the "decorations" for your aquarium: perhaps just an attractive root or some stones in the rear area. Both of these can be purchased at the pet shop. It's more fun of course to collect your own ornaments outside from the natural environment. Limestones, corals and larger

seashells should not be used, however, as they release lime, or calcium carbonate, into the water and create higher pH values and hard water. Gneiss, granite, marble and other primary rocks, on the other hand, are fine as aquarium decor. Before you put them into the tank, wash them very thoroughly using hot water and a stiff brush, but no other cleaning agents. Roots that have not already been lying in the water of a pond or pool will be too buoyant to stay on the ground of the aquarium. These can either be weighted down with stones, or you can soak them in a bucket of water until they are saturated and thus heavier than water. All roots, whether purchased or collected outside, must be freed from dirt, algae, snails and the like. Either wash them under hot water or, even better, boil them for at least ten minutes. Another word on outfitting your tank: usually electric wires and plastic tubing are conducted behind the back wall of the aquarium. In order to hide these and at the same time create the impression of a biotope, you can cover the outside of the back panel with a sheet of paper featuring an appealing scene—it needn't always be a photo of an aquarium!—or with decorative cork, a reed mat, natural jute or other textiles. Aquarium owners with the requisite handicrafts skills can create an elaborate backdrop out of synthetic resin, featuring caves, crags and crevices, which can be mounted inside rather than behind the aquarium. (For more on lighting, see p. 31 ff.)

On the whole, it is not good to stuff the tank too full of apparatus and decorations, because these will only limit the open swimming space for your goldfish. The vegetation should also not be too dense. Goldfish do not always leave the plants to grow in peace. Therefore, some robust, large-leaved or large-stemmed varieties are best. You can obtain these from native waters or purchase them at the pet shop. Hornworts and arrowheads, milfoils and vallisneria are hardy plants that will do well, given sufficient light.

Aquatic plants from domestic ponds must be washed several times in order to minimise the risk of bringing any diseases or undesirable insect larvae into your tank. Goldfish do not need a heated aquarium; they feel at home in temperatures ranging from 10–18 °C, but also tolerate somewhat warmer water. Usually, room temperature is fine. Goldfish do particularly well when the water is well-aerated and filtered. Low, but deep aquariums with a large water surface are better than high, narrow ones, because more surface area means that more oxygen is absorbed into the tank. Pumps and filters of every possible size and capacity are available for purchase as necessary.

If you keep goldfish in your garden pond, they must either be removed in autumn and kept in a cool tank (8–10 °C) for the winter, or they must have the possibility of spending the winter in deeper water (at least 100 cm). It won't hurt the fish if the pond has a centimetre-thick layer of ice on top, but of course you have to make sure all of the water in the pond doesn't freeze! To protect the fish from very cold temperatures, the pond can be covered with reed mats, styrofoam panels or boards, or you can let some water out, so that there is an air layer between ice and water surface of 10–20 cm, which will also insulate well.

Red cap oranda

Goldfish like a varied diet

Feeding goldfish is no problem, at least with regard to type of food. But it is important to make sure the animals get the right amount. Goldfish will eat anything that comes their way! They are big eaters and, as omnivores, will eat both living and dried food in huge quantities. It is therefore advisable to only give them as much food as they can eat within a few minutes, maximally a half hour. If you can manage it, it's best to give the fish two or, even better, three smaller meals a day, making sure that no food is allowed to sink to the bottom

Bubble-eye

and between the stones, where it can no longer be eaten. Besides the fact that the goldfish will get unhealthily fat if given too much food, the resulting large quantities of excrement and uneaten, decaying food will render the water cloudy and toxic.

As we said, goldfish eat both vegetable and animal foods. You should provide both in turn. The vegetable foods include a dry feed specially developed for goldfish, available in flakes, rods, cubes and tablets. It contains all of the vital vitamins and minerals, as well as fibre, carbohydrates, protein and fats. Goldfish also enjoy raw or cooked vegetables chopped fine, such as carrots, potatoes and peas, various salads and chickweed, oats and wheat germ. You can feed them meats such as shredded beef or pork meat or liver, bloodmeal or fishmeal, and living or freeze-dried mosquito larvae, daphnia, tubifex, water fleas and insects. The two latter treats can be caught with a net in ponds and fields from springtime to late autumn.

Goldfish need a varied diet to thrive. Even if they show a marked preference for certain kinds of food, you should not stick with that kind only, but make sure their diet includes adequate proteins and fats, carbohydrates, minerals, vitamins and fibre. Feedcubes and flakes that are used commercially to fatten up fish for the market should not be given to goldfish—or only sparingly, two to three times a month.

What happens when goldfish get sick?

Unfortunately, the old saying "as healthy as a fish in water" doesn't always apply to our fish friends. They are just as susceptible as all other living creatures to diseases and disorders. The farther removed we humans are from an animal, genealogically speaking, the more difficult it is for us to recognise and understand its behavioural patterns, including

those that would tip us off to a change in health.

When is a goldfish sick, and how can we discover which disease it is suffering from? If the fish's behaviour changes greatly, if it gasps for air or lets itself fall to the bottom of the tank with fins hanging down, if it stops eating or if spots, dots or fungus can be seen on its body, these are all possible signs of sickness. The causes behind these symptoms are usually not easy to determine, and by the time a disease manifests itself, it is often too late for treatment. As soon as you have the feeling that a fish is not acting quite normally—compared with its usual behaviour—you should immediately remove it from the community tank and put it in a small aquarium somewhere quiet. This has the threefold effect of reducing the risk of the other fish being infected, giving the sick fish some peace and quiet to aid possible recovery, and making it easier for you to observe it closely and treat it if necessary. Going to the veterinarian is usually not very helpful—because not many of them know anything about fish diseases. It's a better idea to ask the personnel at the local public aquarium, or a knowledgeable pet-shop owner, for advice. Ideally, of course, you should have these telephone numbers and addresses on hand at all times, so you don't have to spend

Buffalohead or lionhead

Information

Ask your dealer about the capacity of the various pumps and filters, for example the hourly turnover rate. When in doubt, always opt for the higher-performance apparatus in order to have some reserves if necessary. Devices that both filter the water and also supply the tank with oxygen via a plastic tube that ends in a diffuser are especially recommended.

Red fantail

precious time searching for them when you have an acute illness on your hands (see also p. 114 ff.)

Where do baby goldfish come from?

From healthy, full-grown and reproductively mature parents—of course!

If you have a pair of these on hand—they should be at least two years old—then breeding is not too difficult. The chances of success in the community aquarium are not high, however, because goldfish eat both eggs and brood, hardly giving any of the young a chance to grow beyond infancy. A better bet are specially prepared breeding tanks, which are 50–60 cm long and 30–40 cm high and wide. You don't need to add any gravel or stones or roots, but rather just a few fine-leaved water plants in pots. A lamp and a filter with oxygen supply complete the technical set-up. Then all you need to do is put the breeding pair or a female and two males into the prepared tank. Usually, you can tell which fish are ready to mate by their behaviour in the community tank, for example when the males start to chase their females and these display bellies that are growing rounder day by day (with accumulated eggs). If you then place these fish into the breeding tank in the late afternoon, where the water temperature is between 16 and 20 °C, and the water level is lowered to about 15 cm in the evening, chances are good that the fish will spawn the next morning. The male chases his mate through the vegetation, and in the process the female expels several hundred, even a thousand, tiny, nearly transparent eggs, which stick to the leaves of the plants. The male then pours his milt over the eggs to fertilise them. Now all you need to do is remove both parents from the breeding tank and put them back in the community aquarium. But if they haven't spawned, then leave them together for a few more days and change the water temperature every 12 hours by +/– 2 °C or 3 °C; or you can put a dividing wall between the male and females for two or three days and then remove it again. Both this separation and the fluctuation in water temperature can exercise a positive influence on spawning behaviour. At the latest by the third or fourth attempt, reproduction should be successful.

Since goldfish do not care for their young, but are instead spawn eaters, they are not needed for raising the fry. Simply keep the temperature in the breeding tank at about 20 °C—if necessary with a tube heater equipped with a thermostat—and aerate the water intensively (but without causing a strong current) in order to ensure a good oxygen supply. At this temperature it will take from 50 to 60 hours before the young hatch. They will immediately attach themselves to the aquarium walls or to plant leaves and stay there, just two to three millimetres long, for about two days, living off the remainder of their yolk sacs. Once these have been consumed, they will set off in search of food. You can feed them special baby goldfish food, or give them *infusoria* (one-celled or slightly larger microscopic animals) and freshly hatched brine shrimp *nauplii*. Both infusoria and brine shrimp eggs can be purchased in pet shops, and the later hatched in normal saline water. The fry should be fed small portions several times a day. The small goldfish, which are not yet golden-red or butter-yellow but instead an almost transparent greyish-brown, grow amazingly fast. After just a few days they can eat larger live feed such as *daphnia* (water fleas) and also finely pulverised fish-food flakes.

At the latest after eight days you should undertake the first partial water change. About one quarter of the tank's contents should be siphoned off using a hose, the opening of which must be covered with a piece of nylon stocking or other finely woven fabric in order not to throw the

Comet

Red telescope-eye (left) and calico telescope-eye (right)

Information

Important conditions for goldfish breeding include adequate aeration of the breeding tank and a water level no deeper than 10–12 cm, so that the fish can easily swim to the surface. A constant temperature must also be maintained, as well as sufficient light (12–14 hours a day).

Kois (Cyprinus carpio)

babies out with the bath water! The water removed from the tank should be replaced with fresh water which has been allowed to stand for two to three days in a plastic bucket, or which has been prepared for the fish with a commercially purchased water conditioner. The greatest care must be taken when adding the new water to the tank. The best way is to put the bucket on a chair so that it is higher than the tank and conduct the plastic hose from the bucket into the tank, sucking on the end to get the flow of water started. You can place the end on a handful of glass wool or a flat stone to reduce the turbulence and make sure the tiny young fish don't get whirled around too much. This type of water replacement should be carried out every six to eight days—depending on how many fry are living in the tank—and there should not be more than 2 °C or 3 °C difference between the water temperature in the tank and that of the fresh water being added.

Of course, all of the young fish will not survive. You should therefore check the tank several times a day and remove the dead ones, along with the water plants in their pots. But first make sure that no living goldfish are hiding amongst the leaves! At two months the little ones will have grown to about 3 cm, and after six months to 5 or 6 cm. If there are a great many offspring, they might have to be divided up between several tanks. More than 25 animals measuring 3 cm in length should not be kept in a 60 x 40 x 40 or 30 cm aquarium. When the young goldfish are six months old, they will have shed their youthful colouring and will look like "real" goldfish. You can keep the most beautiful ones for future breeding—as long as you have enough room—and try to sell the rest to garden centres, pet shops or private goldfish keepers. You won't really make much of a profit—but that is hardly the reason why most of us keep these beautiful and serene guests from ancient China.

By contrast with breeding in the aquarium, breeding in a garden pond or pool cannot really be controlled or undertaken in a deliberate fashion. In the summer any young that have survived the cannibalism of their parents and other adults will appear in the pond and develop into finger-long adolescents. If the garden pond gets too full, the surplus animals will have to be removed. However, it is against the law, and often dangerous for our domestic fish fauna, to simply dump unwanted goldfish into any pond and lake in the vicinity. They could end up crowding out the species naturally inhabiting our waters, as well as encountering conditions under which they themselves cannot survive.

Koi (Cyprinus carpio)

Goldfish have been bread in large quantities in Japan since the sixteenth century, but, as we've learned, they are not really a Japanese fish, but rather stem from China. The koi, however, is another story. Koi were selectively bred from Japanese coloured carp and have by now replaced the goldfish in many garden ponds. Kois can grow to 60 cm and longer, and are therefore not really suitable for indoor aquariums—unless, of course, you have room at home for a 3,000-litre tank...

Kois are easy to distinguish from goldfish: they have clearly visible barbels, or whiskers, at both corners of their mouths, just like our domestic carp. Kois are available in every conceivable and inconceivable colour and pattern. Many have a reddish white, light yellow, blue or red background colour. Scales in grey, black, red, orange and silver are distributed over their entire bodies in such a manner that no fish ever looks exactly like another. The Japanese have established colour standards for koi encompassing a very broad scale, from silver metallic, to turquoise and multi-coloured, to black.

There are standard ways of describing the colour patterns, such as pinecones, tortoiseshell, netlike, reflective, with wave effects and three-coloured. In some especially valuable, selectively bred fish, the colours as well as the patterns on the back and head will be particularly conspicuous and intensive. This is attributable to the fact that koi are kept almost exclusively in ponds and are thus always observed from above. This factor is taken into account when choosing breeding lines.

Koi breeding is easy

Koi are fed just like goldfish, although, with their large size, they can eat even greater quantities. Here, too, you should be sure that little food remains uneaten and is allowed to spoil in the water. There are hardly any uniform rules when it comes to the amount of fish that can be kept in one pond. Koi are social fish, which do not need any "personal space" or their own territories. You might see 30 or 40 of them swimming together in a narrow area without becoming aggressive or chasing one another. The rule of thumb is that a koi of about 50 cm in length needs at least 100 litres of water. As soon as you see the fish regularly coming up for air on a normally warm day, you can assume that the pond is overpopulated and the oxygen supply no longer meets the needs of the fish. You can then either reduce the population or instead add some extra oxygen to the tank on hot summer days, distributing the gas with an air stone. This will also bring some movement into the pond or pool, which in turn will help the water to take up even more oxygen from the surface.

Since koi often burrow in the ground, aquatic plants do not stand much chance with them—apart from water lilies and duckweed. Therefore, there is no need to concern yourself with aquatic vegetation when keeping koi.

Information

Although kois can reach a substantial size and are thus not suitable for most aquariums, they are easy to keep if you have a garden pond available. The only requirement is a minimum water depth of 150–160 cm, especially in the colder months. You will hardly have enough space to bring the kois into the house for the winter, so they will have to be able to spend the colder months outdoors. Hence, a certain depth is absolutely necessary for ensuring that the water temperature does not sink below 5–6 °C. The colder the air and the lower the temperature of the water drops, the deeper the fish will sink into the pond. At water temperatures of below 10 °C, they hardly eat anything any more, like the goldfish, but they also conserve their energy. Therefore you don't have to worry that they will starve.

European Dwarf Fishes

In our domestic European waters there live not only valuable food fish such as trout, perch and pike, but also smaller species with no commercial value, but which nonetheless belong to the ecosystem of a stream, river or lake and can play a major role in shaping this habitat. Almost all of these generally unimpressive-looking fish are dwarves that grow only to about 5–8 cm, and more rarely up to 15 cm long.

In our climes, as well as in southern, south western and south eastern Europe, there are considerable fluctuations in air and water temperature with the change of seasons. While the highest temperatures reached in shallow waters on the hottest days of the year are about 30 °C, the lowest temperatures are around freezing—a range that is about ten times as wide as that found in the tropics. Coldwater fishes could thus also be kept in a heated aquarium without harming them in the short term. However, for their reproductive cycle they require lower water temperatures to get them into mating mood. In addition, many of these species have high to extremely high oxygen requirements, which they can hardly fulfil in warm water (oxygen dissolves much more readily in cold water than it does in warm water).

Let's take a brief look at a few of the native fish species that are appropriate for coldwater aquariums and those that we might be able to purchase or catch during a holiday to other European countries. We strongly urge you, however, to observe the environmental protection laws in each country. You may need to obtain a license to catch some of the endangered domestic fish species. Before catching any fish, it's therefore necessary to obtain information from the local environmental protection or state authorities on whether you are permitted to keep a certain species in your aquarium or backyard pond.

The four best-known domestic small fish species that can be kept and bred well in aquariums are the bitterling, the stickleback, the minnow and the belica.

The bitterling (Rhodeus sericeus)

The bitterling is native to broad sections of Central and Eastern Europe, reaching to the Caspian Sea, Greece and northern Turkey. It lives in shallow lakes and slowly flowing streams with rich vegetation. Bitterlings are usually found in schools. They reach a length of 5–8 cm and are easy to keep and breed in an aquarium, as long as you keep a few

Gudgeon (Gobio gobio)

living freshwater or swan mussels in the tank with them. These are required for the female for laying her eggs. During spawning, she will extend an ovipositor measuring several centimetres in length and deposit about 50 to 60, or sometimes up to 100, eggs into the breathing openings of several mussels. The male follows immediately behind, shedding his milt into the mussels as well. When the mussel sucks in water, the eggs are then fertilised within it.

Protected from enemies, the eggs develop within the mussels' gills, and the young only leave their shelter once they have consumed their yolk sac and have grown to about 10 mm.

Bitterlings primarily eat plants of all kinds with only moderate quantities of animal food. They should be kept at room temperature, which should not go lower than 20 °C during breeding, as the eggs and young will otherwise require much longer to develop.

The three-spined stickleback (Gasterosteus aculeatus)

The three-spined stickleback, which grows to about 4–8 cm and occasionally up to 11 cm, makes an ideal coldwater aquarium pet, with very interesting brooding behaviour. This species is native to wide areas of Europe, ranging from Iceland to southern Italy, Spain and the Black Sea, and has developed a migratory saltwater form that lives in coastal waters. The freshwater stickleback lives in similar areas to the bitterling: vegetation-rich shore regions of standing and slow-flowing waters. When they are not breeding, sticklebacks are very lively school fish. When spawning, the male's colours undergo a striking change; he is transformed from a drab brown animal to an exotic beauty, with a bright red belly and bright greenish blue dorsal area. Starting in March, the males occupy breeding territories at the bottom of shallow water, and build a nest there out of plant

parts held together by a sticky saliva secretions. With his courtship displays, the male entices several females to his nest, where they release their eggs. In this manner, 300–500 and more 1.5-mm eggs are collected. The male tends to these alone, fanning fresh, oxygen-rich water over them, picking out and destroying any dead eggs, and very aggressively driving off other males and fish species that come too close to his nest. Depending on the water temperature, the young hatch in from six to ten days and

Young grass carp or white amurs (Ctenopharyngodon idella)

Three-spined stickleback (Gasterostreus aculeatus), males

The water must be quite clean and well-supplied with oxygen, because otherwise the fry will develop poorly or not at all. In tanks holding 150 litres or more, three to four males and the corresponding number of females can be kept. Their breeding and territorial behaviour can then be observed particularly well, and you will never get bored watching them. However, if some males are being chased too relentlessly by others, you will have to remove the underdogs and put them in a more peaceful tank, or let them go again. A member of the stickleback family that lives in our local waters is the nine-spine stickleback (*Pungitius pungitius*). He differs little from his relative in terms of care and breeding. However, he does not build his nest on the ground but rather hangs it in a water plant. The number of eggs he collects is smaller—usually no more than 80 to 100—and they take longer to develop.

The minnow (Phoxinus phoxinus)

The minnow genus is only represented in our waters by two species, the lake or swamp minnow (*Phoxinus percnurus*) and the Eurasian minnow (*Phoxinus phoxinus*). The latter is especially interesting for our coldwater aquarium. It is very widespread throughout almost all of Europe, only missing in northern Scotland and Scandinavia, in most areas of Spain, in Portugal, as well as in Italy south of the Po River.

Minnows are very active school fish that live mostly in shallow waters and the shore areas of meres and lakes, but can also be found in mountain streams at up to 2,000 metres, as well as in murky, brackish water. Their habitat has little vegetation and they prefer a ground cover of sand and pebbles. They like to hide between stones, overhanging banks and the massive roots of willows and alders lining the banks. They grow up to 6–10 cm, sometimes even to 12 cm, and they are an inconspicuous grey-brown or

Biotope for minnows

Minnows
(Phoxinus phoxinus)

soon go off on their own. They live off tiny shrimps, worms and water insects—while the older animals also eat fish broods and eggs.

In a 50–60-liter aquarium you can keep one male and three to five females at temperatures ranging from 12 to 20 °C.

olive-brown to green colour, with darker spots and a glowing metallic longitudinal stripe.

In nature minnows eat only live food that they find in the water, as well as on the surface.

Mating season begins around April and ends in July. The spawning males and females usually make their way to pebbly spawning grounds, and each female expels up to 1,000 eggs, which are then fertilised by one or more males and left to meet their fate. The eggs sink to the ground and develop in one or two weeks, depending on the water temperature. The young fry grow quite slowly and do not reach reproductive maturity until their third or even fourth year.

The minnow does well in a coldwater aquarium and, thanks to its liveliness, is an enjoyable pet. For 4–5 fish the tank should be no smaller than 50 litres, with a pebbly bed and only a few plants, as well as hiding places such as hollow rocks, flat stones layered over one another to create crevices and caves, and perhaps some roots. Good filtration with an air pump and plenty of water circulation is required, in particular if you would like to breed the minnows. Both males and females display small light-coloured spots, which are known as the spawning rash, in the neck region in the spring. This is not a sickness, but rather indicates that the animals are ready to spawn if they encounter the appropriate conditions.

The belica (Leucaspius delineatus)

Another low-maintenance coldwater fish from our native waters is the belica, which—like the minnow and the bitterling—belongs to the large order of carp (Cypriniformes). Belicas grow up to 8 cm long, have a bluish silver colour and are quite a serene school fish.

Belicas can be found from the central to the eastern parts of Europe between the Rhine and Volga Rivers, where they live in shallow moor ponds, meres and lakes. They are not found at altitudes over 200 metres, nor in flowing waters. They eat every possible insect in the water or air as well as their larvae (for example mosquito larvae, which flourish in warm standing water).

In aquariums, the belica is a quite nondemanding pet, preferring sandy or pebbly ground and requiring very few water plants. A combined filter/air pump apparatus is recommended in order to prevent too many toxins from accumulating in the water.

Young minnows schooling

*Belica
(Leucaspius delineatus)*

Information

April and May are the main spawning season for the belica. The females spin long, spiral strands around plants, to which the eggs are attached, and the male looks after these by keeping the plant in motion to ensure good water circulation. After eight to ten days the young hatch. They live off their yolk sac for the next 48 hours and then go out to hunt for microscopic food. After just one year they have reached reproductive maturity, and will live for three to four years.

Pike (Esox lucius)

Other domestic fish species

There are at least two dozen more fish species found in our waters that can be kept in aquariums with relatively little effort. The least effort is required for members of the whitefish or carp family (*Cyprinidae*), while slightly more work is entailed by the salmon, pike and perch families (*Salmonidae, Esocidae* and *Percidae*). The former family includes the minnow, belica, tench, rudd, sneep, dace, chub, bitterling and roach.

The latter families encompass, among others, the river, rainbow and lake trout, salmon, char, grayling (all of the *Salmonidae* family), pike, ruffe and pike-perch or walleye. Most of these species, however, attain lengths for which the average tank is simply too small. In addition, salmon, pike and perch require extremely high-quality, clear and oxygen-rich water, which is quite expensive to maintain. Some of them are also sensitive to higher temperatures, which means that anything warmer than 20 °C can already cause some problems. Cooling water down, however, is far more difficult than heating it; there is no cooling tube comparable to the widely available heating tube. All in all, the species cited here are simply not fit for the beginner, but should instead be reserved for the specialist.

Foreign Coldwater Fish

A smaller number of species that can be kept in coldwater aquariums originates in northern America (as far south as the Mexican highlands), and others from China and Southeast Asia. They are not always easy to obtain, but perhaps your pet retailer can give you some addresses, or you can find some sources listed in an aquarium magazine. Some interesting varieties, including some ideal coldwater aquarium fish, are the sunfish (*Centrarchidae*), and the egg-laying and live-bearing toothed carp families (*Cyprinodontidae* and *Poeciliidae*). We have already encountered many members of these rather large fish families among the warmwater fishes.

Sunfish— guests from northern America

The North American sunfishes in particular make ideal aquarium pets. Some of them had already reached our shores during the nineteenth century, been released into our domestic waters, and were able to make a place for themselves there (as is the case with the rainbow trout, likewise from North America). However, sunfish are not able to withstand cold winters as well as our native fish species. They have to be taken out of the garden pond in late autumn and kept in a cool cellar for the winter. If instead you keep them in an aquarium— and most species are well-suited for this—you will not have this problem.

The size of the various species ranges from about 4 cm for the pygmy sunfish (*Elassoma evergladei*) and 60 cm to a maximum of 75 cm for the largemouth bass (*Micropterus salmoides*). Although large species don't grow quite as long in an aquarium as they would under natural

conditions, keeping them in an aquarium is still tantamount to cruelty to animals. The sunfish are strikingly beautiful, usually quite colourful fish, every bit as attractive as their warmwater counterparts. Their background colour is often a light chocolate-brown, and some display interesting patterns of stripes or spots. Bright white or iridescent spots and lines ornament their bodies and fins, and, when mating, some turn dark blue or a brilliant bright red.

A few of the 30 or so existing species are available in stores and are appropriate for the coldwater aquarium. These include the pumpkinseed sunfish (*Lepomis gibbosus*) from the eastern USA. This fish was imported into Europe over 100 years ago and released into many standing bodies of water. Since it only grows to about 10–12 cm, at the most 15 cm, it can be kept well in a 150-litre tank. An especially appealing sunfish is another species from the eastern USA, known as the diamond, banded or little sunfish (*Enneacanthus obesus*), which grows from 6–10 cm long. The closely related blackbanded sunfish (*Enneacanthus chaetodon*) also makes a lovely-looking pet. The latter is however not quite as easy to care for as the other sunfishes. Although it tolerates low water temperatures down to about 5 °C, it is sensitive to temperature fluctuations. The water exchanges that should be carried out every two weeks must be done carefully (with water of the same temperature that has been let stand for three to four days in a plastic bucket). The blackbanded and pumpkinseed sunfish are good candidates for a garden pond, because they both tolerate water temperatures close to freezing. The other varieties, in contrast, should not be kept in water colder than 10 °C because they are native to subtropical zones of North America. Feeding most sunfish is easy. They are predators and, at least while they are getting used to their new environment, require live feed such as tubifex, water fleas, daphnia and mosquito larvae. But

they can usually be accustomed to freeze-dried and frozen feed, or even to animal-based flaked food—as long as you give them enough time and the transition from live to other food is fluid.

Some species, for example the pygmy sunfish, can be bred without difficulty in captivity, as long as they are kept cool in winter (10–12 °C) and otherwise at room temperature. In some species both parents tend the eggs and young, in others the males only, and in still others there is no brood care whatsoever.

The water should be near neutral in pH (around 7) and have medium hardness

Pumpkinseed sunfish (Lepomis gibbosus)

Pointed-mouth molly (Poecilia sphenops Valenciennes)

Persian minnow
(Aphanius mento)

American flag fish
(Jordanella floridae)

These fish comprise two families, both of which are extremely popular with aquarium owners: the egg-laying toothed carps (*Cyprinodontidae*) or killifish, and the live-bearing toothed carps (*Poeciliidae*). In the chapter on warmwater fishes we will describe some of these species in more detail. In this section we would just like to point out that some of these species also live in more temperate zones, namely in the eastern part of the USA as well as in the Mediterranean region.

Coldwater species are usually not quite as brilliantly coloured as their tropical relatives, but the males especially can take on a striking blue, red or multi-coloured spawning dress when courting. The species native to temperate zones can be kept and bred well in coldwater aquariums, and some can even be kept outdoors in a garden pond from spring to autumn, where, under the right conditions, they will reproduce on their own. However, in case you then run out of room, you should not simply dispose of the superfluous animals in the next pond or lake. Most species cannot survive our cold winters—and the others would upset the delicate ecological balance in our climes, as has often been the case with other kinds of animals, more notably mammals.

The European varieties that you can easily catch yourself while on holiday at the Mediterranean (after checking the local laws and obtaining any necessary licence, of course) include the two egg-laying toothed carp species, the Mediterranean killifish (*Aphanius fasciatus*), which lives in both the European and North African Mediterranean regions, especially in brackish water, and the Spanish toothcarp (*Aphanius iberius*), which lives not only in Spain, but also in the north western region of North Africa. This fish can be found only in fresh water lakes and ponds. Both of these are quite inconspicuous fish, only 5–6 cm in length, which do very well at room temperature. Water temperatures

(about 10 °dH) and should not be changed too frequently. In the wild many sunfish live in the standing water of ponds and meres, which do not have much of a fresh water supply. Plants in the tank should be restricted to the back wall and one of the sides, leaving the fish 60–70 % of the tank as open swimming space. Lighting of medium strength, for ten hours a day, is best.

The toothed carp—often very colourful and usually small

Another good kind of fish for the coldwater aquarium is the toothed carp.

of about 10–12 °C do not harm them; on the contrary, in the spring when the water naturally gets warmer, they are prompted to spawn.

Other egg-laying toothed carps that can be kept in a tank are the American flag fish (*Jordanella floridae*) and the bluefin killifish (*Lucania goodei*). Both come from the south eastern USA. The former is probably the most widespread cold-water killifish. It grows up to 6 cm long and is not only at home in Florida, but also on the Yucatan Peninsula all the way down to Mexico. The first of these were imported into Europe some 80 years ago. The American Flag Fish can be kept in a smallish tank about 50–60 cm long at water temperatures of around 20 °C. For breeding, however, the water will have to be about 4–5°C warmer.

Now and then, particularly appealing species arrive in Europe from eastern and south eastern Africa. These cannot be kept in the garden pond, but are suitable for a tank at normal room temperature, that is at temperatures of about 20–22 °C. These species include for example the gorgeous bluefin notho (*Nothobranchius rachovii*) from Mozambique, which exhibits a bright spawning dress of blue and red with black dots, and the very delicately coloured blue-green large-finned lampeye (*Procatopus nototaenia*) from western Africa. Both of these are a bit more demanding to care for, but are more brilliantly coloured than the diverse European and North American toothed carps.

The live-bearing toothed carp family also has a few members that can be bred in coldwater aquariums. These were originally only found in the New World, but were later introduced into many countries in Africa and Asia. Some of these are excellent mosquito or mosquito larvae exterminators, helping to keep these pests under control.

Live-bearing toothed carps bear live young rather than laying eggs, as their name indicates. These fry are at once able to swim on their own and must be watched over closely by their parents so they aren't eaten by other fish. The most well-known live-bearing toothed carp is the guppy (*Poecilia reticulata*). Although these can be kept in coldwater aquariums from about 18 °C, we will take a close look at them when we discuss warmwater fish, because they do best at slightly warmer temperatures (from approximately 20 °C), which are also required for successful breeding.

Lower temperatures are just fine, on the other hand, for the variable platyfish (*Xiphophorus variatus*) from southern Mexico and Guatemala—namely as low

Bluefin killifish (Lucania goodei)

Guppy (Poecilia reticulata) breeding form

Information

Coldwater fishes are not available from every aquarium store, so you will usually have to obtain them from private owners and breeders. They will of course know their fish well and will be able to put together a detailed feeding plan for you. They can also give you advice on water quality, such as the pH value and water hardness (dH). If you purchase fish with a view to breeding them, you should also ask the seller about the required breeding conditions, including water temperature, and how to match pairs correctly (in some species each female requires the attentions of several males, and in others one male is enough to fertilise the eggs of four, five or even more females), feed mix and quantity, and anything else that might require some specialised knowledge.

Coldwater aquarium

as around 15 °C—and the quietly attractive Corfu toothcarp (*Valencia letourneuxi*) from southwest Greece. The latter can survive winters as cold as 10 °C—which even improves the likelihood of breeding as compared with constant water temperatures. *Gambusia affinis*, the mosquitofish, can also do well at 10 °C, depending on the subspecies. This is one of the gambusia species that are used throughout the tropics as an effective exterminator of mosquitoes and their eggs and larvae, and which has also been imported into European waters. Besides live food, they also eat algae (as do many toothed carps) and vegetarian flaked food. If you put Mosquitofish in a tank with dense vegetation and a temperature of about 22 °C, the females will bear between 40 and 50 live fry. It is then advisable to remove either the parents (which is usually easier) or

the young from the tank. Otherwise, the fry will disappear one by one into the stomachs of the parents as well as of other adults.

We would like to conclude our discussion of coldwater aquarium fishes with one of the smallest fish in the world: *Heterandria formosa*, called the least killifish but also referred to as mosquitofish like its close relative, the gambusia. This tiny fish from Florida and South Carolina grows only to 2 cm (males) or 3.5 cm (females) and can thus be kept in small tanks up to 30 litres. It loves dense, fine-leaved vegetation and is a very peaceful, unimposing and low-maintenance pet. It readily breeds even for beginners who have little knowledge of pH and water hardness. Like most toothed carps, these fish eat live feed such as water fleas and artemia, but also accept algae and finely pulverised dry food. Over a period of eight to ten days the female bears two to four minuscule fry per day, which immediately disappear into the thick jungle of leaves and are usually left in peace by the older animals. After four to six weeks another spawning cycle follows. If you wish to promote spawning, it's best not to let the water temperature sink below 20 °C.

A Suitable Coldwater Aquarium

Coldwater aquariums are similar to warmwater ones in both construction (panorama, all-glass or frame) and size. The technical equipment required is also for the most part the same—with one exception: you don't need a heater. The only time you would need this is if you keep your fish in a basement that is not adequately heated in the winter. On the other hand, it is sometimes favourable for the breeding biology of some fish when they experience a colder period in winter, just like in their native waters. Some species need this temperature drop to come into mating condition. The temperatures required for this, from 8 to 12 °C, can easily be maintained in an unheated but well insulated cellar. For other coldwater fish, for example, those that come from sub-tropical regions, these temperatures would be too cold. A tube heater can be used to heat their water to 18–22 °C. Fish who need a hibernation period in the winter should also be given shorter periods of light during that season than in summer. After all, they come from temperate zones where the length of the days changes with the seasons: ranging from about 16 to 17 hours of daylight in the summer, to only 8 to 10 hours in the winter. If the room is shared by coldwater fish that you would like to breed, their water temperature will have to be raised, and they will need quite a bit more light (see also p. 31 ff.)

There is one thing you should be clear on before you set up an aquarium and purchase fish for it: coldwater fish are by no means less demanding or any easier to care for than their warmwater counterparts—with the single exception that they usually do not require that the water be heated.

(see also p. 31 ff.)

> ## Information
> *The diet of coldwater fish is not much different from that of their warm-water relatives. Some of them are herbivores, others need live or at least animal-based feed (frozen or freeze-dried), while still others are omnivores that live on algae, flakes and tablets as well as all kinds of living and dried feed.*

*Minnows (*Phoxinus phoxinus*) in a coldwater aquarium*

Warmwater Fish
Living in Fresh Water

People walking into pet or aquarium specialty shops are usually captivated by the rows of display tanks teeming with colourful and often comical-looking fish. Even a neophyte will notice right off that these are strictly warmwater fish—the heaters and thermostats quickly give that away. In fact, most tropical fish come from places where the mercury seldom dips under the 20 °C mark and the water temperature hardly fluctuates more than 3 °C or 4 °C all year long.

As we mentioned in the earlier chapters, warmwater fish are nowadays easier to keep, care for and even breed than their coldwater counterparts—those who inhabit water at temperatures under around 20 °C. Everything is standardised: aquarium heaters are matched to the tank size, and a thermostat allows one to set the water temperature never to deviate more than a degree or two in either direction. Filters take care of purifying the water, and aerators ensure adequate oxygenation. Lamps closely approximate daylight in both intensity and composition, and, thanks to test kits and chemicals, your exotic fish can enjoy almost exactly the same water chemistry that they would find in their natural habitat.

Then there's the fish food industry! It offers every form of nourishment imaginable—from prepared foods that claim to supply fish with all the necessary fibre, vitamins and minerals—to the special live foods one must serve in the early stages to newborn fry up to 2 mm in size.

Thus, keeping warmwater tropical fish is now at best a craft, and no longer an art. "Take one part this and two parts that," and "Insert tab A into slot B" is basically the name of the game. There are two or three dozen tropical fish for whom it's almost impossible to do anything wrong. These will thrive even if they receive an hour less daylight than in their native environment, are inadvertently deprived of a feeding, or if their water's pH isn't maintained perfectly.

Since this book is meant as a guide for aquarium beginners with little or no knowledge of fish-keeping, we will generally limit our discussion to those fish that can be kept, cared for and bred without the owner needing to hold a doctorate in fish studies. Later, though, we will mention a few showpieces and

Dwarf gourami (Colisa lalia), red variety

treasures, such as the discus and some rare cichlids from South America and East Africa. This is meant both to give readers an appetite for more, and to assure them that with a bit of experience, they'll be ready to take on even trickier charges.

Both the animal and plant kingdoms are organized according to a comprehensive system known as scientific classification. All animals are to a greater or lesser degree related, and so they are grouped based on their relationship to others, providing specialists with a means of classifying the different species. These groups are ranked hierarchically into genus, subfamily, family, suborder, order, etc.

Some genera and families are quite small, consisting of only a few species. Others have many hundreds of members, such as the egg-laying toothed carps, of which nearly 500 different species exist, spread out over virtually the entire world. The species covered in the coming pages all belong to one of the following families (Latin designation ending in -ae) or orders (Latin designation ending in -formes or -toidei):

- Characins or true tetras *(Characidae)*
- Darters *(Characidiidae)*
- African tetras *(Alestidae)*
- Whitefish or carps *(Cyprinidae)*
- Loaches *(Cobitidae)*
- Catfish *(Siluriformes)*
- Egg-laying toothed carps *(Cyprinodontidae)*
- Live-bearing toothed carps or live-bearers *(Poeciliidae)*
- Cichlids *(Cichlidae)*
- Labyrinth fish *(Anabantoidei)*

Many species today still have no common names. These are referred to exclusively by their Latin names in fish-keeping circles. Some examples are cichlids, toothed carps and labyrinth fish. Among species that do have common names, some go by different names in different places. For any species that

doesn't have an explicit common name, we have used the Latin designation in order to avoid confusion. Latin names are usually given in a form known as "binomial nomenclature": two words written in italics. The first, capitalised name designates the genus; the second, uncapitalised name designates the species. For example, *Pterophyllum scalare*

Angelfish in a beautifully planted aquarium with South American fish

X-ray tetra

Neon tetra

have no trouble locating vast amounts of more or less specialised literature on the topic of aquarium fish.

Characins (Characidae)

This extremely large fish family, comprising over well 700 species, is found mainly in tropical South America. There are varieties, however, ranging from northern Patagonia to above of the Tropic of Cancer (Mexico). Many of its species are among the most commonly collected tropical fish worldwide, and some of these are well suited to beginners.

Characins are predominantly small- to medium-sized fish, running from about 5 cm to a maximum of 25 cm in length. In normal tanks, the larger varieties never reach the size of their free-swimming cousins, and top out at approximately 10–12 cm. In these cases, the fish will often not display the complete splendour of a fully-grown specimen. For our aquariums, with an average capacity of 80–100 litres, only the smaller (4–6 cm) species are appropriate. In keeping with the fishes' home waters, the pH of the aquarium water should range from acidic to mildly acidic, or between 5.8 and 6.5. Soft water (peat-filtered, for example) is important, as are good plantings and a darker-collared tank bed. Roots, small stone structures (no limestone!) and lushly verdured nooks are also appreciated.

Many American characins are schoolers, and so are seen to their best advantage in single-species tanks. In adequate numbers—ten or more individuals—they do make a nice addition to larger mixed-species tanks (80–100 cm in length). They all like clear, clean, well-aerated water, kept in circulation with a diffuser or airstone. The more common species are trouble-free to breed, with some producing so many young that at some point one hardly knows what to do with them all.

is the Latin name for the well-known freshwater angelfish. A close relative, *Pterophyllum altum*, is more commonly known as the altum angelfish. By using Latin names, fish enthusiasts the world over can know what species they are talking about, even if they speak completely different languages.

The first half of this book is devoted to the keeping, care and breeding of the different species. As indicated in that section, we will now go into special considerations, as well as tank size and configuration, feeding and required water temperatures. Since there isn't room to cover even the most widely-known species, we have grouped the more closely-related fishes together, not least to avoid repetition. Any reader interested in exploring more detailed information on specific species will

Neon tetra
(Paracheirodon innesi)

The small (up to 4 cm long) and strikingly coloured neon tetra is one of the best-known and most widespread of all tropical fish. The first specimens were brought from eastern Peru to France 50 years ago, and from there made their way into our aquariums. In contrast to other species that were sought-after and fashionable for a while, only to drop almost or completely off the radar screen, the neon has managed to remain in continuous favour among aquarists. Many dealers sell them by the dozen; here we advise caution, as these fish often come from industrial breeding facilities and never attain their lifespan potential of three to four years.

An even lovelier, though more demanding variety is the cardinal tetra (*Paracheirodon axelrodi*). This species has the dark red colour running the entire length of the body, while in the neon it extends forward only as far forward as the anal region.

The neon is very much a schooling fish, and should be kept in groups numbering at least 12 to 15 individuals, either in medium to large mixed-species tanks or in smaller (60–80-litre) single-species ones. Its preferred environment includes a dark substrate, dense plantings with swimming room in the foreground and mildly acidic, soft water kept at around 25 °C. Also important is rather muted lighting, which one achieves by stocking the aquarium with floating plants. The neon will eat both dry and live food, and is generally happy to take freeze-dried organisms, which make a good substitute in winter for live food.

Black tetra or black widow tetra
(Gymnocorymbus ternetzi)

This is an attractive tetra from central South America which will grow to a good 5 cm and inhabit the middle and upper depths of an aquarium. Calm and peaceful, the black tetra likes to live in schools, and is much less picky about water than the neon. Though it prefers more diffuse lighting, it can be kept in brighter tanks as long as cover in the form of dense perimeter vegetation is available. Breeding is relatively trouble-free, and brings numerous offspring.

As omnivores, black tetras do prefer live food, but in a pinch will get along quite well on fish flakes and freeze-dried food. Similar in upkeep and only slightly more challenging is the silvertip (*Hasemania*

> **Tip**
> *It is highly recommended to avoid buying neons smaller than 2.5 cm—pay a little more for larger ones instead.*

Black tetra or black widow tetra (Gymnocorymbus ternetzi)

tetra, a variety 7 cm long out of central South America, between Argentina and eastern Brazil. Water hardness and pH are of little concern to this species, and it accepts temperatures from as low as 20 °C to almost 30 °C. It can be kept in small numbers in a mixed-species aquarium. An omnivore, *Hemigrammus caudovittatus* is especially happy to dig into water plants of all types; one must therefore use only sturdy, hard-leaved plants in the tank, as this fish will quickly decimate any of the more delicate vegetation.

From Guyana comes another member of the same genus, the glowlight tetra. A red band runs from above its eye down the whole length of its small, 4-cm body. The band is shown to its best advantage in subdued light, by which the fish seems to glow from within, especially when seen against a dark tank bed. They are kept in small schools in mixed-species tanks with water at pH-neutral or slightly lower and a temperature around 24 °C. For nourishment, they take micro organisms or the smallest fish flakes.

Another variety often found in stores is the head-and-taillight tetra (*Hemigrammus ocellifer*) which comes from northern and central South America. As with many species of *Hemigrammus*, *H. ocellifer* is a small fish, reaching scarcely more than 4 cm in length. It is best displayed in schools and is very comfortable in mixed-species tanks. It has care and maintenance needs similar to those of other species of *Hemigrammus* and *Hyphessobrycon*.

The last of this genus is the somewhat more sensitive firehead tetra (*Hemigrammus bleheri*) from the northern regions of South America and from Brazil. This 4-cm-long fish is a quite lively one that will swim around all day long, and should mingle only with other equally lively species. It wants soft, rather acidic water that gets changed regularly in order to keep nitrate levels down (therefore always prepare fresh water

Head-and-taillight tetra
(Hemigrammus ocellifer)

False rummy-nose tetra
(Petitella georgiae)

nana), a beautiful, although not very colourful tetra, which originates in eastern Brazil. Like many of the so-called blackwater species, it prefers a dark aquarium bed with good plantings that still leave it sufficient room for swimming.

Buenos Aires tetra
(Hemigrammus caudovittatus)

Another fish very well suited to the beginning aquarist is the Buenos Aires

with a water conditioner from a specialty shop). The firehead will do very well under these conditions—however it is not the easiest species to breed.

Redeye tetra
(Moenkhausia sanctaefilomenae)

This fish with the nearly unpronounceable name can be found in many mixed-species tanks, because one will encounter almost no problems caring for it. It does well in schools and is content with water ranging from mildly acidic to mildly alkaline and of any hardness. Water temperature should not fall below 22 °C. At an overall length of 7 cm, it counts among the larger tetras, though in smaller tanks it won't grow much larger than 5 cm. The redeye is an omnivore, and therefore not difficult to feed— it will keep hale and hearty on a diet of fish flakes, daphnia, tubifex worms and insect larvae. Even a novice will have no problem breeding this species. One places the breeding pairs in small, 30–40-litre tanks furnished with floating plants and an artificial spawning substrate (a green nylon spawning mop). After the eggs are laid, one must separate the adults from them, or they will soon eat them all up. After about 48 hours (depending on water temperature) the fry will emerge. In another 24–36 hours, they will be ready to eat the finest fish flakes, and in a week they will take tiny live food.

Flame tetra
(Hyphessobrycon flammeus)

In this genus comprising around 70 member species, the best known is the flame tetra, which is native to river waters in the Rio de Janeiro area. The first specimens came to Europe almost 80 years ago, and have since proven to make exceedingly easy-care pets—one can hardly do anything wrong to them. The flame

tetra is at its best in mildly acidic, soft water at or slightly above 24 °C. Breeding is easy and can indeed inundate one with offspring. Most aquarium supply dealers will not accept fry from private breeders, however, for fear of introducing disease.

A truly beautiful fish is the ornate tetra (*Hemigrammus bentosi*), a 4-cm variety with several recognised sub-species, differentiated mostly by the colour of their fins. Even more vibrantly coloured is the serpae tetra or blood characin (*Hemigrammus callistus*), which is produced almost exclusively on Asian breeding

Redeye tetra (Moenkhausia sanctaefilomenae)

Buenos Aires tetra (Hemigrammus caudovittatus)

farms, and, as its name suggests, is dark red in colour. It displays a characteristic black marking behind the gill cover, as well as a black dorsal fin. The flag tetra (*Hemigrammus heterorhabdus*) is somewhat less striking. A native of the central Amazonas region, it has a red-black stripe that runs the length of its body down to the base of the tail, reminding one vaguely of the neon. It seldom gets bigger than 4–4.5 cm and is best displayed in larger schools (15 or more individuals).

*Blood characin
(Hyphessobrycon serpae)*

Darters (Characidiidae)

Not all ichthyologists are in agreement on the classification for darters. To simplify matters, we will go with the widely accepted benchmark work by Günther Sterba, *Süßwasserfische der Welt* ("Freshwater Fish of the World", 1990). The darter family numbers some 60 members and is restricted to a region of the New World stretching from Panama to Uruguay. Most of its species stick close to the bottom, establishing small territories and not forming schools. For aquarists, the most interesting of the family's five genera is *Nannostomus*, which they group under the collective name of pencilfish. Its ranks include several very beautiful species, all a mere 4–6 cm long, and all favourites of experienced aquarists, who like to keep them in mixed-species tanks.

Most of these species are more demanding in terms of water quality than our recommended beginners' varieties. The pH must be held at just under neutral, a value best achieved through peat filtration. A water hardness of around 3.5 °dH will appeal to the fish. It is important for the pencilfish that these values not fluctuate. They can share a tank with other docile species that aren't too large, and will keep mostly to the middle depths, preferring a dense plant cover in which to spend the day. Not until evening do they become active and go out foraging, at which time you can feed them small live food and small fish flakes. One of the most beautiful species of *Nannostomus*, and one appropriate for beginners with a little more experience, is the golden pencilfish (*Nannostomus beckfordi aripirangensis*), from northern South America. This fish does best in a tank 60 cm or more in length, with dense vegetation accompanied by a thin layer of floating plants. Two even more challenging species are the three-stripe pencilfish (*Nannostomus trifasciatus*) from Brazil and the tiny dwarf pencilfish (*Nannostomus marginatus*) from northern South America. The dwarf pen-cilfish should be kept either in a single-species aquarium or one that has only other very small varieties; otherwise it will become timid and hardly ever show itself in open water.

African Tetras (Alestidae)

Compared to South American varieties, African tetras are not always so easy to maintain, and very few could be considered beginner fish. They are therefore a much less common sight in our aquariums than their South American cousins. They are at their happiest in a long tank with thick plantings kept to the back and ends, allowing them plenty of free swimming room, through which they will roam unceasingly. Their water should be soft and mildly acidic, at a temperature between 23 °C and 27 °C. Good aeration is essential to the African tetras' well-being. Since they are only irregularly bred if it all, most species are only available from importers, and are thus quite expensive. These fish stand out not so much for colour variety or distinctive marking as for their beautiful metallic hues—now brilliant, now subdued, depending on how the light strikes them. Many of these 8–10-cm species are truly superb specimens. Kept in schools, they make for a marvellous sight that can make you forget even the most colourful of South American fish. Above all, we recommend the Congo tetra (*Phenacogrammus interruptus*), native to the Congo River region. From the same family come the yellowtail tetra (*Hemigrammopetersius caudalis*), the red Congo tetra (*Alestes imberi*) and the 12-cm longfin tetra (*Alestes longipinnis*). These all make interesting schooling fish, and are best kept in an aquarium at least 80 cm—but preferably 100 cm—in length. The tank bed should be rather dark, and overhead lighting tempered with floating plants (an exception is the longfin, who appreciates

bright light). These tetras are omnivores with a particular fondness for live food. In addition, they can take appropriate-sized fish flakes, and some, such as the Congo, will help themselves to the more tender water plants.

An aquarist with a bit of experience caring for fish will find great delight in a single-species tank of African tetras.

Carp
(Cyprinidae)

With the exception of Oceania, Central America and South America, this fish family is found the world over, and numbers over 1,500 species—divided among five subfamilies and nearly 300 genera. For aquarists using heated tanks, only two subfamilies are of interest:

- the barbs (*Rasborinae*) and
- the carps (*Cyprininae*).

Included in these groups are a good dozen of the most popular and easiest-to-care-for aquarium fish, species that number in the millions worldwide and which we'll cover at length in the com-

Blue Congo tetra (Phenacogrammus interruptus)

Information
The flame tetra's diet consists of an alternating variety of live and dried food, though it can also subsist on fish flakes as a main food source. The same is true for the species of Hyphessobrycon introduced here. They all like diffuse lighting (easily achieved with floating plants), a darker aquarium bed and tankmates that are not all too feisty.

haviour is better demonstrated in greater numbers. In choosing an aquarium size, you should start from a basic minimum of 50–60 cm, enlarging as fish size and population dictate. Dense plantings are lovely, as long as you can leave a clear swimming area in the front centre of the tank. Barbs and carps keep mostly to the middle and upper water strata and, as many of them are excellent jumpers, you must cover the tank securely to avoid losing fish. They have low to moderate water analysis requirements, doing well in mildly acidic water that isn't too hard. Depending on their origins, these subfamilies inhabit water at temperatures ranging from 20 °C to 26/28 °C. Now we'll discuss several varieties that you can keep in mixed-species tanks with relatively little effort.

Redstripe rasbora
(Rasbora pauciperforata)

Giant danio
(Danio aequipinnatus)

ing pages. The recommended species are predominantly small fish that in the wild would measure 5–10 cm, but in captivity tend to run a bit smaller. Many species are schoolers who are shown to better effect and whose distinctive be-

Zebra danio
(Brachydanio rerio)

This remarkably lovely fish, only 4–4.5 cm long, comes from eastern India and is especially content in schools of ten to 15 individuals. It is lively, and will spend all day long swimming back and forth the length of the tank with its companions. They get along fine in the presence of other species, but in suitable numbers make a beautiful sight in a tank of their own. Feeding them is likewise trouble-free. The zebra danio is an omnivore; equally content with fish flakes and tablets or dry and freeze-dried food, it will especially appreciate a live meal.

Giant danio
(Danio aequipinnatus)

Not as common a find but just as easy to keep is the 10-cm long giant danio from western India and Sri Lanka. They should be kept in schools numbering at least six or seven fish in a mixed-species aquarium measuring at least

80 cm in length. Due to their vivacious-ness, they'll want plenty of space for swimming. Their preferred water temperature is between 22 °C and 24 °C and their nourishment needs match those of the zebra danio. With a varied diet, they will hold up for many years in your aquarium.

Harlequin rasbora
(Rasbora heteromorpha)

The bulk of species belonging to the genus *Rasbora* is made up of unimpressive, not very colourful fish having a native range from the tropical regions between India, Sri Lanka and Southeast Asia up to sub-tropical China. The harlequin rasbora is among the loveliest and most commonly kept species in our aquariums. With a body length of 4–4.5 cm, it can be kept in a smaller tank—50–60 cm will suffice. Keep in mind that it wants to live in a school to be happy and will make a lively denizen of the middle tank depths. It shuns both garish lighting and a light-coloured tank bottom, but will especially enjoy an environment with a cover of delicate floating plants and a substrate of brown or dark-grey gravel. The tank plantings should be confined to the back and side walls, leaving plenty of swimming space, which the Harlequin will use to its fullest. Given mildly acidic to acidic (pH around 6.0) and soft (not over 8 °dH) water, it is not difficult to keep. Breeding, however, is quite challenging for an inexperienced beginner. The harlequin takes a diet like that of the zebra and diant danios.

Eyespot rasbora
(Rasbora dorsiocellata)

This is one of those species whose colouring and markings don't pull you in at first sight, but become more impressive upon closer inspection. Depending on how the light strikes it, the eyespot gleams silver-green or silver-blue and the lower part of its eye glows light green. It is a lively-swimming schooler that

does well in a mid-sized tank—upwards of 70 cm—where it will spend most of the day swimming through the spaces between the plants. Its alimentation, however, presents no problem; as an omnivore it will consume live as well as dried food.

Harlequin rasbora
(Rasbora heteromorpha)

Tiger barb
(Barbus tetrazona)

mellow species. It should be kept in a school and given a tank measuring 70–80 cm, with plenty of swimming room in which to let off steam.

Having been kept and bred for a good 50 years, this species now presents a good range of colour mutations, which enjoy relatively great popularity. Like many rugged barbs, this one places few demands on the water, provided it is warm enough—between 23 and 25 °C. Other examples of the genus *Barbus* that can be set up and maintained in the same way are the Chinese or halfstripe barb (*Barbus semifasciolatus*) from south eastern China, the Ticto or twospot barb (*Barbus ticto*) from India and Sri Lanka, and the very attractively coloured and patterned black ruby or purple-headed barb (*Barbus nigrofasciatus*) from Sri Lanka.

Redtail sharkminnow (Epalzeorhynchus bicolour)

This carp was long designated under the genus *Labeo* and was not known by its common name. When the naming conventions were revised, it and some

Black ruby barb
(Barbus nigrofasciatus)

Dwarf or chain loach
(Botia sidthimunki)

Clown loach
(Botia macracanthus)

Tiger or Sumatra barb
(Barbus tetrazona)

This barb will grow up to 8 cm long in its native waters of Sumatra and across Southeast Asia, but seldom reaches past 5 or 6 cm in an aquarium. It is a popular starter fish that is better kept with its own kind than in a mixed-species environment. This is because the tiger is a feisty fish who tends to cause a ruckus in the aquarium and disturb other more

other members of the genus were reclassified as genus *Epalzeorhynchus*. Among owners and in pet shops, you still find the redtail sharkminnow under the name *Labeo*. This beautiful, popular aquarium fish and its close relative the ruby or rainbow sharkminnow (*Epalzeorhynchus frenatus*) both originate from Thailand, grow to 10–12 cm long and are loners. You must keep them in tanks with only their own kind, as they will aggressively antagonise other species and cause unrest. They remain mostly on the bottom, often hiding behind roots and rocks. These sharkminnows will be quite content with a diet of fish flakes, blanched greens and live food of any kind. They are partial to algae—you will always see them grazing along the surfaces of leaves, roots and the aquarium glass. Their water should be rather soft, kept pH-neutral, and be refreshed at intervals where a quarter to a third of the water is replaced every two or three weeks.

Loaches (Cobitidae)

The loaches are an interesting and relatively small fish family, numbering some

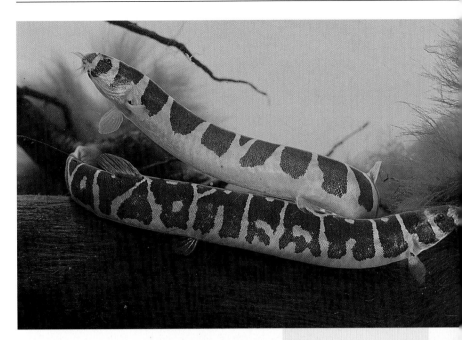

200 species. They are found over broad ranges of Eurasia, in Arabia and in two tiny areas of Africa.

Loaches can attain a maximum length of 30 cm, though they seldom grow longer than 5–10 cm in captivity. They like an aquarium that isn't too bright and has plenty of nooks and crannies in which to hide, and they prefer to live in small groups. One should furnish them with coconut shells and small flower-pots in which to spend the day. At dusk they will emerge to scour the tank bottom thoroughly in search of food. As for water chemistry, they are quite tolerant,

Coolie loach (Pangio kuhlii) and Borneo or Shelford's loach (Pangio shelfordi)

Zebra loach (Botia striata)

151

seeming to prefer mildly acidic, softer water. Loaches do require warmth—the water temperature should not fall below 24–25 °C—and a good supply of oxygen is essential.

Efforts to breed loaches have met with only haphazard success so far; the species one encounters are almost exclusively taken from the wild.

Most loach species have an elongated, almost eel-like body. A few look rather like catfish, though they are not closely related.

Though many are omnivorous, most species prefer live food over mixed or vegetarian fish flakes.

One of the loveliest loaches is the dwarf or chain loach (*Botia sidthimunki*), from northern Thailand and Laos. It grows to only 4–4.5 cm and its lively, mostly diurnal behaviour will best come out if it is kept in schools. As with many loaches, it likes to hide itself in the bottom. We recommend that decaying plant matter be allowed to accumulate in a deeper corner of the tank so it can retreat there for rest or to escape disturbance. For nourishment, the dwarf botia will take small live food and small fish flakes.

A fish three or four times the dwarf's size (up to 15 cm, that is), the clown loach (*Botia macracanthus*), is a popular one with fish keepers. As with the dwarf, it likes to live in a small school. It is peaceable, getting on well with both its own kind and other species. Because it is predominantly active during the daylight and evening hours, one will see the clown loach more often than other *Botia* species. Being an omnivore, it is easy to feed, and though one will quickly discover which foods it likes best, one should be careful not to let the diet become too lop-sided. Occasionally one will come across loaches of the genus *Pangio* (a.k.a. *Acanthophtalmus*) in shops. One example is the coolie loach (*Pangio kuhlii*) from Borneo, Sumatra and Java; another is the half-banded loach (*Pangio semicinctus*) from Southeast Asia. Both live as loners and are predominantly nocturnal, often hiding themselves under rocks and behind roots during the day. One feeds them therefore in the evening, giving them live and frozen food whenever possible as they are not generally fond of fish flakes or tablets.

Raphael catfish
(Platydoras costatus)

Catfish (Siluriformes)

The catfish order is extraordinarily rich in species, comprising more than 2,000 across some 200 families. While the European river catfish can reach an impressive length of 300 cm, many South American varieties only grow to finger-length. One of these, the pretty dwarf cory (*Corydoras gracilis*), is at only 2.5 cm one of the world's smallest fish!

The different species of catfishes are dispersed throughout the world, excepting only Australia, New Guinea and New Zealand. In the northern hemisphere they range almost up to the Arctic Circle; in South America nearly down into northern Patagonia.

Aquarists are chiefly interested in the smaller varieties native to the tropical

regions of Central and South America, Africa and Asia.

Of the almost three dozen catfish families, three furnish the bulk of the order's representation in aquariums:

- the Callichthyid armoured catfishes *(Callichthydae)* from South America,
- the armoured catfishes *(Loricariidae)* from South America,
- the squeakers or upside-down catfishes *(Mochocidae)* from Africa.

While the catfish order is uncommonly rich in species, there are basic similarities across the order in its fishes' characteristics and behaviour patterns. Almost all catfish remain at or close to the bottom, most are peaceable, and in contrast to most aquarium fish, many are nocturnal. This is an important factor in the feeding regimen and for temperature regulation. Nocturnal catfish do not take nourishment until the evening, and anyone who lowers the water temperature by several degrees at night (for example, by using a timer) should not keep or care for nocturnal catfish.

Many catfish are vegetarians, and are generally quite efficient at keeping algae growth in check. Most are brought

into the aquarium to scavenge decomposing plant material and fish food that have sunk to the bottom. For catfish that prefer live food, it's best to give them the kinds that sink to the bottom, such as worms (tubifex, grindal, enchytrae) or larvae (mosquito, midge). Omnivores will eat a rotation of tablets, flakes, live food and frozen food. As regards water quality and chemistry, catfish are seldom demanding; some come from a natural habitat where the water is turbid, oxygen-poor and brackish. The

Candy-striped pleco (Peckoltia vittata)

Emerald catfish (Brochis splendens)

Leopard cory (Corydoras leopardus or julii)

most commonly available species of armoured catfish and Callichthyid armoured catfish are exceedingly appreciative and make excellent additions to

Common pleco or sucker-mouth catfish

Blotched upside-down catfish

any aquarium. Nearly all catfish like a densely planted tank with plenty of possible hiding places, either roots or different stone structures and any kind of decorations.

As long as the pH and water hardness remain within normal limits, the catfish will do fine. Water temperature should correspond to its native habitat—typically 22–26 °C, but occasionally up to 28 °C.

Some 100 species of catfish are available for tropical aquariums, with more being added each year as they are introduced and bred by dealers and individual aquarists. With such an abundance of species, one can always find the right catfish for the tank, taking into consideration appearance and behaviour (diurnal or nocturnal, flesh- or plant-eating, whether it likes to hide or live out in the open). In the following pages, we will briefly describe some of the more available and easy-to-maintain species.

Cory Catfish are Especially Popular With Aquarists

The best-known genus in the Callichthyid armoured catfish family is *Corydoras*, or cory catfish. About 200 species have been discovered in South American rivers so far. Some 50 have made their way over to Europe; of these about a dozen are regularly kept and bred by enthusiasts.

One such species is the bronze cory (*Corydoras aeneus*), whose habitat runs from Venezuela to central Argentina. It grows to 6 or 7 cm and has a metallic gleam. A good arrangement groups two or three males in a large tank with up to five females. As is the case with most corys, the bronze requires a good deal of live food, but will also take dried. Some are fond of finely chopped hard-boiled egg yolks.

The same is true for the peppered cory (*Corydoras paleatus*), a 5–6-cm variety from central South America. One will often find the albino variety at shops. Like most of its kind, the peppered cory likes to have a variety of hiding places available, such as small flowerpots, halved coconut shells and thumb-sized holes or crevices in rock piles. A recommended way to soften overhead lighting is to introduce floating plants, provided this is appropriate for the other tank inhabitants.

The leopard or three-line cory (*Corydoras trilineatus*) has exceptionally beautiful markings. Native to the central Amazon and various Peruvian rivers, it reaches a length of only 5 cm. *Corydoras*

Sterba's cory (Corydoras sterbai)

Information

Since catfish are predominantly active during the day, they are easy to observe and can be fed in the morning or early afternoon. One can easily breed them in small spawning tanks holding about 20 litres. The young will hatch in five or six days and be ready to take infusoria and the smallest daphnia.

trilineatus should be kept in the company of at least five or six others of its own species, and will get along quite well with these and other tankmates. It enjoys a densely vegetated tank with a few open sand or gravel surfaces in which to dig about.

For someone who wants to care for an especially small catfish, the pygmy corydoras (*Corydoras pygmaeus*) is a good choice. This tiny fish from Brazil gets only as long as the first joint in one's thumb! Contrary to most corys, the pygmy keeps to the middle and upper water depths. It eats miniscule live food such as tubifex worms and daphnia, with fish flakes as a supplement to its staple food.

Also a catfish, but belonging to a different genus, is the gorgeous, silver-green iridescent emerald catfish (*Brochis splendens*). Its native habitat is the upper Amazonas, where it is a very common fish in countless tributaries. At an overall length of 8–9 cm, it is somewhat larger than the varieties previously described. The emerald catfish is gregarious, and should not be kept alone, but rather with a half-dozen or so companions. Only then will it best show its lively and interesting behaviour. It gets on well with other fish, and one follows the same keeping guidelines as with the *Corydoras* species.

Our final representative of the Callichthyid armoured catfishes is the spotted hoplo (*Hoplosternum thoracatum*). It inhabits large stretches of South America's tropical and subtropical river systems, often forming schools of several hundred fish. Growing as long as 18–20 cm, this is a grand catfish that—if one plans to have multiple specimens—will need a large tank that is thick with plantings and offers plenty of hideouts.

The spotted hoplo is active at dusk and therefore should not be fed until late afternoon, when it will happily take live food and tablets alike. Breeding this species is often successful, provided one remembers to remove the female from the spawning tank very shortly after the eggs are laid to prevent her gobbling them all up.

Armoured catfish can reach 50 cm in length!

The second-largest family of the *Siluriformes* order is the armoured catfishes. It probably numbers over 500 different species, of which only a few make their way into aquariums. Although a number of armoured catfish species will do perfectly well in a well-outfitted tank, they have higher expectations regarding accommodation and care than do most catfish. We will therefore stick to a few species that a beginner can keep in a 60–80-cm aquarium with no problem. It is interesting to note that attempts to breed these easy-to-care-for fish have so far met with amazingly limited success. This is a sign that there must be some requirement these fish have regarding feeding, circulation, oxygen, etc. that as yet escapes our knowledge—something aquarists accept as a challenge.

The common pleco or suckermouth catfish (*Hypostomus punctatus*) is an attrac-

Angel squeaker (Synodontis angelicus)

tive species and a relatively easy one to care for. It comes from tropical Brazil, where it can reach lengths of up to 30 cm, but rarely grows past 15–18 cm in an aquarium. It makes a great algae exterminator in any tank, but needs lots of room (an aquarium length not less than 100 cm). In addition to algae, the common pleco will eat all kinds of greens, which should be blanched and sliced thin, and it will happily consume vegetarian flakes and tablets.

A much smaller fish—barely 4 cm long—is the dwarf or golden otocinclus (*Otocinclus affinis*) from Brazil. Of the almost 30 species in this genus, this one seems to be the most popular with aquarists. It is not very picky about water composition, but in nature the fish inhabits lightly acidic, somewhat soft water.

All the *Otocinclus* species have earned a reputation as efficient algae exterminators. In addition, they will eat vegetarian fish flakes and tablets as well as blanched greens; you will quickly discover which greens appeal to them and which do not.

Among the predominantly nocturnal catfish fall the members of the genus *Rineloricaria*, numbering some four dozen species. Some of these are available to aquarists, for example the small-scaled whiptail catfish (*Rineloricaria microlepidogaster*) from tropical Brazil. In the evening, they must be given plant-based flakes and tablets; otherwise they will surely starve if they can't find enough algae. During the day, they prefer hiding themselves behind roots or in grottos, or dig themselves into the tank bed.

Squeakers, or upside-down catfishes (*Synodondis contractus*), live in central and western Africa

Many catfish live in central and western Africa

All the previously described species have their origins in South America; however

catfish also inhabit sub-Saharan Africa and are found along the Nile River up to its delta. Around 150 species belong to the squeaker family, some of which one will encounter in aquariums. They are nocturnal creatures, which limits their value as a display species. This is

Malawi squeaker (Synodontis njassae*)*

unfortunate, as many species are interesting and lovely fish.

One of these is the blotched upside-down catfish (*Synodontis nigriventris*), a native of the Congo River. It especially likes to forage for live food on the undersides of roots and plants. It can be fed it mosquito and midge larvae, which it skims from the water surface while swimming upside down. Given water temperatures between 22 °C and 25 °C, dense plantings and a gravel bottom that isn't too light-coloured, this species will do well and live to a ripe old age. One of the few members of this family that are often active during the day as well is the orange-striped squeaker (*Synodondis flavitaeniatus*), likewise a Congo River native. In the aquarium, it will grow to 10–12 cm (in the wild up to 20 cm) and does well in a mixed-species tank with a capacity of at least 130–150 litres. Though the care and keeping of this species present no problem at all, it is unfortunately not readily available in pet shops.

Egg-laying Toothed Carps
(Cyprinodontidae)

African lyretail (Aphyo-semion splendopleure), different colour variants

Egg-laying carps are found everywhere but Australia and Oceania, with their main areas of proliferation being in Africa and South America. On both continents, they are largely missing from

climes below the Tropic of Capricorn. In North America, they occur mostly in the east and north east; in Europe, within the Mediterranean lands; in Asia they inhabit a 200-km band along the coast, including Japan. These fish are also known as killies or killifish.

This extremely large family—comprising about 500 different species—boasts some of the most beautiful of all aquarium fish, though the preponderance of species hardly grow larger than 5–6 cm. Since the great majority of killies do not make good beginner fish—indeed some should only be kept by experts—less space is devoted to them here than one might expect considering their numbers. Still, there is quite a number of species for those who have already earned their first fish-keeping spurs. Among them are several varieties of African lyretails (for example *Aphyosemion* sp.), most of which come from West Africa, with a few originating in Zaire.

They inhabit the shallow waters of the savannah, which often completely disappear during the dry season. The adults will then die, while the egg-bound embryos survive in the damp mud to hatch when the rains return. For most, their lives only last until the next dry season.

Killifish are suitable for mixed-species tanks only under certain conditions, and are best kept in small groups in a tank of their own. For the smaller species, a 50- to 60-cm tank will do; the larger, 8–10 cm long species will want a 70-cm tank. Killifish are not too picky about water chemistry, but are happiest with mildly acidic water at an overall hardness of between 5 °dH and 10 °dH. Recommended water temperatures range from 22 °C to 25 °C or 26 °C. For most killies, a regular routine of partially replacing their tank water has been shown to be of great value, even though in the wild they are accustomed to spending weeks in a stagnant puddle.

More important than water chemistry for the egg-laying toothed carps is the ar-

Blue gularis
(Aphyosemion sjoestedti)

Blue-eyed livebearer
(Priapella intermedia)

rangement of their aquarium. It should provide plenty of cover, such as roots and rocks with grottos, or stacks of flat stones, as well as a darker sand bottom or peat layer in which to hide.

One should also cover a large portion of the water surface with floating plants, as wild killies often live under embankments and in thickly grown, shallow habitats.

The most favourable gender arrangement for single-species tanks consists of one male with several females. Many species can be bred without too much effort. They lay their eggs either in the soft (for example peat) bed of the aquarium (substrate-spawners) or on fine water plants, Java moss (*Vesicularia dubyana*), or on an artificial substrate such as wool fibres or the like (mop-spawners).

The substrate-spawners are somewhat more labour-intensive to breed than the

mop-spawners. For the former, one must simulate the dry season called for by their evolutionary programming. To this end, the eggs must be packed in damp turf and, depending on the species, be set aside for two to five months. After that they are placed back into the aquarium, and then the young emerge within anywhere from a few hours to a few days.

With mop-spawners the task is easier. The adults affix their eggs to water plants and the young hatch in 14 to 20 days. In their native habitat, killies take their nourishment almost exclusively from live food. This comes mostly in the

Killies or Killifish

Common name (Latin name)	Native habitat	General info
Lyretail, Cape Lopez lyretail (Aphyosemion australe)	Cameroon, West Africa	easy to keep, mop-spawner, 5–6 cm long
Twostripe lyretail, two-banded killie, ted lyretail (Aphyosemion bivittatum)	western Africa	easy to keep, mop-spawner, 5–6 cm long
Red-barred powder-blue killie (Aphyosemion bualanum)	western into central Africa, savannahs	easy to keep, mop-spawner, 4.5–5 cm long
Jewel killie (Aphyosemion exiguum)	western Africa	easy to keep, mop-spawner, 4–5 cm long
Gulare, deltafish, yellow gularis, red-spotted gularis (Aphyosemion gulare)	Nigeria, western Africa	easy to keep, substrate-spawner (turf), 7–8 cm long
Redtail notho, Gunther's nothobranch (Nothobranchius guentheri)	Tanzania, eastern Africa	quite easy to keep, substrate-spawner, 4,5–5 cm long
Golden panchax, Playfair's panchax (Pachypanchax playfairii)	Seychelles	quite easy to keep, mop-spawner, 9–10 cm long
Longfin killie, featherfin panchax (Pterolebias longipinnis)	Brazil, central South America	for advanced aquarists, substrate-spawner, 10–11 cm long
Peter's killie (Aphyosemion petersii)	western Africa	for advanced beginners, mop-spawner, 5–6 cm long
Green rivulus, Cuban rivulus (Rivulus cylindraceus)	Cuba	easy to keep, mop-spawner, 5–6 cm long
Dogtooth rivulus, Mexican rivulus (Rivulus tenuis)	Mexico	easy to keep, mop-spawner, 3.5–4 cm long (!)
Brown-spotted killifish (Profundulus punctatus)	northern Central America, southern Mexico	easy to keep, mop-spawner, 11–12 cm long
Jamaican killifish (Cubanichthys pengelleyi)	Jamaica	quite easy to keep, mop-spawner, 4–4.5 cm long

Please note: Be sure to cover the aquarium—many toothed carps can jump!

form of insects, which they catch on the water's surface, but they will also eat these insects' larvae that grow in pools and meres. In the same way, they require live food daily in the aquarium. Occasionally one can get them to accept dried or frozen food, but more often than not they will refuse anything that doesn't move or act like prey. North American and Mediterranean egg-laying toothed carps also need plant intake in the form of dried food and algae.

Most killifish are quite short-lived. Those that are native to drought areas have a lifespan of less than a year, and the others live two or three years.

Green sailfin molly (Poecilia velifera)

*Redtail notho
(Nothobranchius
guentheri)*

Pair of guppies

Live-bearing Toothed Carps
(Poeciliidae)

The native habitat of the live-bearing toothed carps is the New World, from the north eastern and eastern United States, through Mexico and Central America, and down into Uruguay. Over the years, however, they have been introduced into many parts of the world, partly as a mosquito-control measure (as has been done with the colder-water species *Gambusia affinis*). From the family Poeciliidae come some of the most widely distributed aquarium fish. Four good starter types for the novice aquarist looking to gain some experience are: guppies, swordtails, platys and mollies. These breed with no need for interference from their keepers, who will often wake up in the morning to discover that their fish have once again produced a brood. Helmut Stallknecht has described in detail the care and breeding of live-bearing toothed carps (see p. 86–113). We will

On the following pages we will introduce a few types of killies that are appropriate for the advanced beginner to keep and breed. Their reproductive biology is such that these varieties aren't perennially available, meaning one must sometimes wait weeks or months to acquire them.

therefore be brief and limit ourselves to some general commentary on a few species that are easiest to care for.

The guppy
(Poecilia reticulata)

This small-toothed carp from northern South America is certainly the best known of all warmwater aquarium fish. The male grows to a mere 3 cm, the female up to 6 cm. The former displays all the colours of the rainbow on his body and fins and exists today in so many colour mutations that even the experts can no longer keep track of them all. Most colour varieties are now bred in Southeast Asia and are imported in great numbers into Europe, where they are often used as food for larger species and for other animals.

Guppies are fine with water temperatures from around 18 °C to just under 30 °C. They like slightly alkaline water (pH around 8) and an overall hardness between 2 °dH and 10 °dH. Bear in mind

Rainbow killifish or bluefin notho (Nothobranchius rachovii)

Fancy guppies

Information

*The first swordtail
specimens came to
us shortly after the
turn of the century.
As the wild form
already exhibits
numerous colour
mutations, breeders
had no trouble in
quickly coming up
with a dozen new
varieties. The most
popular are the green,
yellow and red varie-
ties. As with other
aquarium species,
swordtails in captivity
are significantly smal-
ler than those found in
the wild. On average,
the males reach a
length of 5–6 cm, the
females a bit more.
In the case of Xipho-
phorus helleri, it's easy
to distinguish the
sexes: in the male,
the lower portion of
the tailfin has an
elongated, sword-like
shape, though it is
neither pointed nor
sharp. A well-known
aspect of these fish is
the sex-change from
female into male. In
fact, it is not a true
change of gender but,
rather, a case of de-
layed development
in which the late-
developing male re-
sembles a female for
its first one to three
years before outwardly
displaying its maleness
in the form of the
"sword" fin.*

Various swordtails

that heavily bred varieties are somewhat more sensitive to water chemistry,
and it is a good idea to start off with
hardy stock acquired from an experienced breeder. The tank should measure at least 40 x 30 x 30 cm. Guppies
want a thickly planted aquarium with a
certain amount of swimming room in
the front. They will also appreciate a
roof of floating plants such as water
fern (*Salvinia*), as long as sufficient
overhead light comes through into the
tank. They can inhabit either single-
species or mixed-species tanks. In the
latter case, one must avoid mingling
them with particular species—Siamese
fighting fish, for example—that may be
tempted to nibble at the males' tre-
mendous dorsal and tail fins.
Their diet should be an alternation of
live food and various fish flakes.

The swordtail
(Xiphophorus helleri)

The wild swordtail is native to southern
Mexico and Guatemala, where it is broad-

ly distributed in four subspecies. As for water chemistry, the swordtail has the same needs as the guppy, likewise for the tank plantings. It is for the most part a peaceful fish, and will leave even smaller species alone.

However, when several adult males are competing for the favour of a female, this can bring about quarrels that culminate in a single male establishing dominance over the others. A normal reproductive cycle lasts from five to six weeks, and depending on her size, the female will give birth to anywhere from a handful to a hundred of live, fully-developed young.

Swordtails have a diet similar to that of guppies: live food, plant-based and other flakes (the staple), tender greens and algae-covered water plants.

The platy
(Xiphophorus maculatus)

A member of the same genus as the swordtail, the platy is also native to Mexico and Guatemala. It is about the same size as the swordtail and can be found commercially in just as many colour mutations—but with the platy the dominant colours are consistently dark red, orange and yellows. These fish often display black spots or patterns, and black fins. They make ideal tenants for a problem-free mixed-species aquarium and are less aggressive than male swordtails. Swordtails and platys are easy to cross-breed with each other, as are the other *Xiphophorus* species.

All the particulars given for guppies and swordtails regarding tank setup, water temperature and chemistry, and feeding hold true for platys as well. The young become sexually mature after four months, and breeding is easy. In the interest of thoroughness however, we should mention the variatus platyfish (*Xiphophorus variatus*), which exists in many variants—the orange, yellow and blue platys are a few basic examples.

Keeping and breeding requirements match those of the standard platy.

The molly
(Poecilia spenops)

The fourth of these extremely easy-to-handle live-bearing toothed carps is the molly, which in the wild inhabits river deltas and brackish estuaries extending from Texas and Mexico down into Central America. It likes water that is slight-

Variatus platyfish
(Xiphophorus variatus)

ly salty—about one teaspoon of cooking salt per 8–10 litres of water—conditions that will not appeal to other species. Thus if one plans to provide the molly a brackish environment, it should be in a single-species aquarium.

Breeders have managed to produce a small number of colour mutations in mollies as well, though only two have really caught on: the black molly, a coal-black variation, and the golden molly; a third more rare type is the speckled molly.

Mollies from the wild can be kept at a temperature of 18 °C or 19 °C (room tem-

Red wagtail platy
(Xiphophorus maculatus)

perature), while the bred forms are considerably more delicate and want the water to be at least 22 °C.

In contrast to the previously mentioned live-bearers, most mollies are vegetarians, and will graze on algae they find in the aquarium in addition to being fed plant-based fish flakes, universal flakes (as the staple) and vegetarian tablets.

The cichlids (Cichlidae)

At around a thousand different members, the cichlid family is one of the most species-rich of all freshwater fish. Some 200 are native to Central and South America, most of the rest are in sub-Saharan Africa, and a handful come from southern India and Sri Lanka. The cichlids from the great lakes of the East African Rift Valley are far and away the most popular and widely collected in their family.

Cichlids have conquered a variety of habitats, from the streams and rivers of the rain forests and savannah to the bottomless Lake Tanganyika and Lake Malawi and the relatively shallow Lake Victoria. They live in a variety of water conditions: from very salty to murky and brackish water, in shallow and stagnant pools or in slow-flowing rivers, and some only in protected coves. A few economically significant African species have been brought into South America and South East Asia, where some have escaped and established themselves in waters they found to their liking.

The smallest cichlid, *Lamprologus kungweensis*, measures less than 40 mm whereas the largest, *Boulengerchromis microlepis*, a yellow colossus, can reach a length of 75–80 cm. The species suited for aquarium life range from 10–15 cm in length, and the majority require a tank capacity of at least 100 litres.

One can easily distinguish cichlids by their shape

The vast majority of cichlids have a typical perch shape: rather flat and high-backed, not often elongated. A trait common to almost all of these fish is their conspicuous and exceedingly large dorsal, anal and tail fins. Many varieties have well-developed ventral and pectoral fins as well. In addition to being known for their striking colours and markings, cichlids are intriguing to aquarists because of their fascinating reproductive behaviour.

In considering their spawning habits, cichlids are divided into two groups: open-breeders and close- or hidden-breeders. The former lay their eggs in hollows on the bottom, then both adults stand guard together over the eggs, attacking any fish—even other species—that pass too near the spawning ground. The latter either lay their eggs in natural grottos and empty snail shells (cave-breeders), or the female takes them into her large mouth and keeps them there while they

*Borelli's yellow dwarf cichlid (*Apistogramma borelli*)*

Cichlid habitat: Amazon

Information

There are two cichlid varieties that are particularly popular with aquarists: the angelfish and the discus. Many enthusiasts consider the latter the "king of aquarium fish." We will describe both in some detail, though they—especially the discus—are not exactly species one would recommend to an aquarist with no experience.

Firemouth cichlid (Thorichthys meeki or Cichlasoma meeki)

mature (mouthbrooders). Maturation time depends on water temperature and quality, among other factors. In mouthbrooders, the time to hatching can be anywhere from 11 to 40 days, after which the young emerge from the mother's (or in rare cases the father's) mouth and swim out in search of food. Over the next few days, they will promptly retreat to the parent's mouth at the first sign of danger.

Keeping cichlids

Many cichlids have the reputation of being aggressive towards their own kind and other species alike. They must therefore be kept in a single-species tank, either in pairs or in small family groups. Some types are avid burrowers who will plough up the entire tank bed; for these you can set up a tank with larger pebbles or rock fragments, omitting sand that might cloud up the water. Others cannot swim by a plant without indulging themselves in a nibble or two. They are capable of devouring the most beautifully-planted aquarium bare in short order. These types are kept in plant-free tanks stocked with roots, large rocks and stacks of flagstones to provide hideouts.

Such cichlids are not recommended for beginners. However, there are many types that are easy to keep in either single or mixed-species tanks, that will not dig up the tank bed or gobble up all the plants, and aren't too difficult to breed (see p. 93).

For smaller cichlids, go with an aquarium that holds between 80 and 100 litres. Almost all species not hailing from the previously mentioned African lakes can be kept in planted tanks. The tank bed should consist of 3–4 mm gravel and the tank decorated with an assortment of non-calciferous rocks. Bogwood roots make a good addition to an aquarium, too. One can buy them at pet shops or go out and take them right from the moor—just be sure to give them a good scrubbing! Many cichlids are quite tolerant concerning water temperature, and are fine with a range from 24–27 °C or 28 °C. They are likewise not too sensitive about acidity or hardness; a pH value around neutral (7.0) is good, and the hardness can range between 5 °dH and 20 °dH, according to species. The dealer or breeder can give you more specific indications—varieties that have undergone generations of breeding often have a higher water tolerance than those taken from the wild.

The cichlids' menu

As we've learned, some cichlids take great delight in eating the loveliest and most tender water plants. Luckily they do not take their sole nourishment this way, or things could get expensive. The majority of cichlids are omnivorous and thus eat live, freeze-dried and frozen food as well as vegetarian flakes and fresh greens.

You should provide them with a rotating menu so as to avoid monotony. Otherwise, certain cichlids might under some circumstances help themselves to one of their smaller tankmates... On one day, for example, you can feed them plant-based flakes along with fresh, well-washed greens, finely chopped spinach, dandelion leaves, chickweed and other tender, wild plants that one gathers from March into October in meadows and forest fringes.

The next day the fish can have live foods such as daphnia, tubifex worms and mosquito or midge larvae, all of which one can get from spring into fall at pet shops or gather oneself from ponds and meres. In the latter case, the live food must be given multiple washings before being fed to the fish. It is a good idea not to give the fish more than they can consume in a few minutes—even better is to feed them a smaller amount three times daily than a large quantity at once.

On the third day one can stick one or two food tablets to the side of the aquarium in addition to providing minced meat, small bits of fish, prawn and shellfish, and frozen food (thaw it thoroughly first!).

A fasting day once a week won't do the fish any harm—on the contrary, the day after they go without food they will be more likely to accept food that they might ordinarily turn down. In this way, one can broaden the menu possibilities while better preparing the fish for those times when live food is more difficult to come by.

That being said, young fish shouldn't be put on a diet, as they won't have developed enough fat reserves and so can die if they aren't fed daily.

Cichlids of South and Central America

The discus
(Symphysodon discus)

The discus is known to aquarists as the "king of the freshwater fish," and we will describe it in considerable detail in

spite of it the fact that it is not a beginner's fish. It is a member of the very large cichlid family (*Cichlidae*), which today are among the most popular and prevalent of aquarium fish. The first specimens were introduced in Europe in 1921, but it was several decades before they were successfully bred in captivity. Nowadays most of the fishes come from European and Asian breeding stock, though more and more fish keepers are asking for wild ones.

Fairy cichlid or lyretail lamprologus (Neolamprologus brichardi)

Brown discus (Symphysodon aequifasciatus axelrodi)

169

Heckel discus (Symphysodon aequifasciata)

The wild discus makes its home in South America

Both the Heckel discus (*Symphysodon aequifasciata*) and the green or turquoise discus (*Symphysodon aequifasciatus aequifasciatus*) are native to the river tributaries of the central and lower Amazon region. There they appear in schools when they are not spawning, and are a food source for the area's indigenous peoples.

In Peru, the discus has been abandoned by humans as a source of food and it has propagated itself so well that huge numbers are caught for export to North America and Europe.

Long and tall, but thin as a blade

The discus' body is, as one might guess from its name, disc-shaped. It is very thin (1–2 cm) and depending on species and subspecies, runs in length from 8 to 25 cm, with an almost equal height. In the aquariums typically used for these fish—200–300 litres—they often fail to attain the size of the wild forms.

The wild discus' basic colour ranges from light to chocolate brown. The head, neck and fins are generally light blue with red dots or streaks, and seven to nine fairly conspicuous dark stripes run the length of the body.

Pet shops and breeders offer discus in countless colour mutations, with such names as royal blue, golden sunrise, red turquoise, cobalt and nura solid red. According to demand, these can fetch quite a hefty price.

Beautiful creatures come at a price

The discus is not a beginner fish! The prospective buyer should already have experience in the keeping and care of less demanding fish before deciding to buy a discus. Even the mass-produced breeds, which by the way come mostly out of Southeast Asian breeding houses, are not cheap. Prices are based on both size and rarity.

The smaller the discus, the less expensive it will be, and the lower its chances of survival. It is generally better to lay out a bit more money and settle for fewer fish. Five to ten specimens will suffice for a 250–360-litre tank. Some rare colours of discus command many times the price of the normal mutations—the prices can go well over 1,000 pounds...

Don't buy an aquarium that's too small

To keep ten fish that might grow to 20 cm each, you will want an aquarium at least 100 cm long, with height and front-to-back dimensions both around 50–60 cm. This corresponds to a volume of 250–360 litres. The tank bed should be soft (no coarse gravel) and not too thickly planted, leaving about half the tank's volume clear for swimming. A few roots and stones—no limestone!—can be added to furnish dens and hideouts for the fish.

For the rest, the discus shuns bright light, preferring a more subdued effect. They can be provided with the desired atmosphere by filtering the lighting through plants that float on the surface,

Information

In the following pages we will present several cichlid species that the novice aquarist can keep and often breed. The latter does not always hold true for the very popular angelfish, however. In the case of the discus, successful breeding has much to do with getting the water chemistry right. But if you pay attention to a few critical factors, you should have success in keeping and caring for them, at least. The discus' beauty and easy-going nature make it one of the most treasured of aquarium fish.

Elongated cichlid (Pseudotropheus elongatus)

*Yellow belly cichlid
(Cichlasoma salvini)*

some fish are happy with and others reject. Purist aquarium keepers are convinced that live food is the only thing for their discus.

Breeding—a specialist's domain

If keeping discus is hardly trouble-free, this holds doubly true when breeding them. During the spawn, the mated pair is quite territorial, and will tolerate no other discus coming near their turf. The female lays her three or four dozen eggs onto plants, roots, or cleaned stones. After two full days, the young emerge, remaining another three or so days at the spot where they hatched before they can swim freely. At this point, they will begin to feed on a secretion produced by the adults' skin. Now they will hang on to the parents' fins for a few days before beginning to venture out a few centimetres, always retreating instantly to the parents' protection at any sign of danger. After a week or two, you can begin to give them the tiniest microorganisms—the food powder that can either be bought in pet shops as "fry food" or gathered directly from ponds and meres. As soon as the young can find food for themselves, they can be separated from the adults so the latter can spawn again and the young can grow without being disturbed. Within about three months, they will have assumed the characteristic disc shape, and at eight or nine months, their adult colour patterns.

for example water fern (*Salvinia*), bladderwort (*Utricularia*) and floating liverwort (*Riccia* sp.).

Two critical factors in keeping discus are the water quality and composition. The water should be mildly acidic (pH around 6.5) and soft (2–3 °dH). Every two or three weeks you should replace 20–25 % of the tank water, making sure to maintain the above values (see p. 34 et seq.).

Corresponding with the native habitat, the appropriate water temperature is 26–28 °C, or just slightly warmer for spawning. If you want to settle the fish down somewhat—often a prerequisite for successful spawning—you can drop the temperature to 23–24 °C, and then raise it to 30–31 °C in the spring.

Special attention must be given to feeding. The discus is a predatory fish, feeding on live creatures in their native river habitat. One can feed them tubifex, mosquito and midge larvae, daphnia and brine shrimp. Various fish food producers offer a universal dry food that

The angelfish
(*Pterophyllum scalare*)

Only a few decades ago, the angelfish was considered a fairly difficult fish to keep, and one that placed particular demands on water temperature and chemistry. Breeding attempts seldom met with success, and then only with considerable effort. The situation has since changed dramatically. Today's aquarium angelfish come exclusively from breeding houses and are hardly more delicate than neons, harlequin rasboras, or flame tetras. They are native to long stretches of the Amazon and its tributaries. As early as 1909 the angelfish was introduced in Europe, where it long remained a rarity. Males and females are nearly impossible to tell apart.

Angelfish like a tall tank, not too deep front-to-back, and with a water temperature between 23 °C and 26 °C. A soft, mildly acidic water is good: pH around 6.5 and hardness no higher than 5 °dH. The aquarium should have very little water circulation and have plantings only at the ends and back. A dozen finger-thick bamboo stalks stuck in a back corner of the tank bed make a nice addition.

Among these, one can plant a group of watermilfoils (*Myriophyllum* sp.), the best being Brazilian watermilfoil (*Myriophyllum aquaticum*), which will grow to a height of 50 cm and enjoys the same water composition as the angelfish.

Two other genera of water plants, burr-heads (*Echinodorus*) and crypts or water trumpets (*Cryptocoryne*), lend themselves to the "Amazon aquarium." Both are favourite spawning surfaces for angelfish.

If you buy angelfish when they are young, i.e. at 3–4 cm, they will get used to each other and live in a school. In contrast to many other cichlids, they don't dig up the tank bed and tear into the plants. They can live in either single or mixed-species tanks. In the latter case, bear in mind that if the tank is larger than 400 litres, the angelfish can develop into magnificent specimens that might, however, pose a danger to smaller species. They are predators, after all, and will go after neons and other

A pair of angelfish spawning

Marble angelfish
(P. scalare)

characins. They eat live, freeze-dried and frozen food as well as fish flakes, all of which are completely palatable to domesticated breeds.

Over the course of their domestication, a great many angelfish mutations have come about, the care and keeping of which are the same as for the normal breeds. Among others, one finds marble, ghost and gold forms of angelfish, as well as black, half-black and albino forms. Angelfish aficionados, however, dismiss most of the bred colours, preferring the natural wild ones.

The genus Cichlasoma

The largest and most species-rich South and Central American cichlid genus is *Cichlasoma*. It includes over 50 species, many of which are kept in aquariums and will reproduce without all too much trouble. They are open-breeders, building nest craters in which the female lays a multitude of inconspic-

uous eggs that blend well with the bottom. The male then fertilizes them, and the two watch over the spawn of some 400–600 eggs, cleaning them and fanning fresh water over them with their fins. They care for their brood well. During the spawn, many *Cichlasoma* species tend to become quite aggressive and nippy towards other fish, so it's a good idea to keep them in their own spawning tank during this period.

Depending on the species, cichlasomas vary in length from 15–30 cm, and so require a minimum tank length of 90–100 cm. Many tend to burrow about and devour the more delicate plants, so one should bear this in mind when setting up the aquarium.

For nourishment, the members of this genus will eat all the foods already indicated for the other cichlid varieties, namely live and flake food of every form. The following species are more or less regularly available and can be kept with no trouble in the appropriate size aquarium:

- Zebra or convict cichlid *(Cichlasoma nigrofasciatum)* from Central America, length up to 15 cm
- Yellow belly cichlid or Salvin's cichlid *(Cichlasoma salvini)* from Central America and Mexico, length up to 15 cm
- Chocolate cichlid *(Cichlasoma crassa)* from the Amazon, length up to 30 cm
- Rio Grande cichlid, Rio Grande perch, or Pearl cichlid *(Cichlasoma cyanoguttatum)* from Mexico and Texas, length up to 30 cm
- Nicaragua cichlid or moga *(Cichlasoma nicaraguense)* from Nicaragua and Costa Rica, length up to 25 cm
- Banded cichlid or eyespot cichlid *(Cichlasoma severum)* from northern South America, length up to 20 cm

The sizes given above are for fish in the wild. Given the space limitations imposed by most fish tanks, one can expect one third to one half of these sizes in cap-tivity. All *Cichlasoma* are open-breeders that lay up to a thousand eggs on cleaned stones. Once the young are hatched, the adults place them on roots or in hollows, keeping a watchful eye on them.

African Cichlids

The genus Hemichromis

Particularly beautiful and coveted cichlids are the dozen or so species in the genus *Hemichromis*, especially the jewel cichlid (*Hemichromis guttatus* or *Hemichromis bimaculatus*). It lives in the tropical regions of thickly forested West Africa, and was brought to Europe for the first time about 90 years ago. This cichlid grows from 8 to 12 cm long and has intensive red colouring with white or blue iridescent dots on the fins or covering the whole body and, depending on the sub-

*Jewel cichlid (*Hemichromis guttatus *or* H. bimaculatus*) with young*

Information

Hemichromis *should be kept in a tank about 80 cm long with corresponding height and width. The water temperature should be 23–24°C and the pH value neutral, i.e. around 7. The fish prefer softer water, approximately 5–10°dH.*

Sulphurhead aulonocara (Aulonocara maylandi maylandi)

species, one or two fingernail-sized dark areas on the sides. The genders are not easy for the layperson to tell apart.

Most of the *Hemichromis* species like to dig in the ground and do not mind if they root out a few plants in the process. The tank bed should therefore consist of larger-sized pebbles, and plants from the robust *Vallisneria* or *Sagittaria* families should be chosen. With regard to food, the same rules apply as mentioned in the general section on cichlids. As an open brooder, the female lays her eggs on a flat stone. The parents then transport the 200–300 eggs to a shallow pit, where they watch over them vigilantly and make sure they get enough fresh water.

The genus Tilapia

In this species-rich genus (about 30) can be found both ornamental and com-

mercial food fishes. The latter play a major role in the food supply in many parts of Africa—for example in the vicinity of Lake Victoria. Some are raised in fish-breeding facilities. When they have reached the size of about 25 cm, they are sold in the market, and in many areas are the only source of protein for the native population.

The tiger tilapia, or spotted tilapia (*Tilapia mariae*), is popular among cichlid fans even though it is rather finicky about water quality. The water should be slightly acidic and soft, not cooler than 25 °C and contain enough oxygen. Since the spotted tilapia is a herbivore, you shouldn't add plants to the tank and will instead have to provide oxygen by means of an air pump and airstone. When full-grown, *Tilapia mariae* cannot be kept with other species and not really with members of its own species either—it's best to keep them as a single pair. The tilapias are open-breeders, which lay be-

tween 1,000 and 2,000 eggs. Both parents watch over the eggs in their pit.

Some species from Lake Malawi and Lake Tanganyika

The best-known and most frequently kept cichlids come from the two East African lakes, Malawi and Tanganyika. In both lakes over 200 different cichlid species can be found, the majority of which are endemic, which means they live nowhere else in the world. The uniqueness of the cichlids in these two lakes is manifested by the fact that they form the majority of all fish in the lakes: in Lake Tanganyika over 70 % of all fish are cichlids, and in Lake Malawi they are almost 90 %!

Both of these lakes have hard water—which is very rare in the tropics—and pH values of 8 to 8.5 (alkaline), with temperatures between 25 °C and 27 °C in the coastal zones. Cichlids stem from ancestors that lived in the ocean and are therefore still tolerant of saline water. In their native seas, the cichlids live primarily in the shallow areas near the shore (called the rock or sand littoral), which is largely devoid of vegetation. One group of species lives in deeper regions up to 120 metres, and another group prefers the surface water of the open lake.

The most interesting species for the aquarium owner are those inhabiting the rock and sand littoral. They are kept in larger tanks, of about 150–200 litres and up. The water must be rich in oxygen and has to be changed frequently (25–30 % of the tank content per week). Also important is strong filtration, since cichlids are hearty eaters and produce a corresponding amount of excrement. Decorations should consist mainly of a dominant rocky or cliff-like backdrop with plenty of caves and crevices. The tank bed should be covered with coarse sand or larger pebbles, and the only plants which have a

chance of surviving are robust, tough-leaved ones from the genera *Vallisneria* and *Cryptocoryne*, and perhaps *Crinum* and *Anubias* as well, which should best be set at the edges of the aquarium.

Here in Europe the *Melanochromis* group, which comes only from Lake Malawi, is the one found most frequently in stores. These include the striped Malawi golden cichlid or golden mbuna (*Melanochromis auratus*), the bluegray mbuna or electric blue Johanni (*Melanochromis johanni*) and *Melanochromis melanopterus*. Two particularly beautiful varieties are the

Electric yellow labido-chromis (Labidochromis caeruleus)

Barred lamprologus (Neolamprologus fasciatus)

Zoologically, the sub-order Anabantoidei are related to the climbing perches. In aquariums, however, they often go by the name of labyrinth fishes. Of the four families in the sub-order, only one is of interest for the aquarium beginner, the bettas (*Belontiidae*), which includes such well-known members as the paradise fish, fighting fish and gouramis. Almost all of the varieties available in stores are easy to keep and care for. They often reach the astonishingly ripe old age—for small fish anyway—of six to eight years. They place relatively modest demands on the water quality, both with regard to pH value (between 6 and 8, i.e. slightly acidic to slightly alkaline) and hardness—depending on the species, between 6 and 20 °dH.

Most of these fish come from the tropical waters of India and South East Asia, which means they require water temperatures of about 25 °C. Some paradise fish from China and Korea can also be kept in a coldwater aquarium, as long as the temperature does not sink below 16 °C. Bettas are usually omnivores. They should be fed with adequate live food for their size, or with food flakes and tablets. You can obtain more detailed information on food preferences from the dealer or breeder who sells you the fish.

In the following section some of the most popular and for the most part low-maintenance species will be mentioned. Most of these can be kept in a community aquarium, but it is important to make sure that there are no fish in the tank that might bite off their thread-like ventral fins.

The Siamese fighting fish
(Betta splendens)

This gorgeous labyrinth fish first arrived in France in 1874, where it found many

Dwarf or three-striped croaking gourami (Trichopsis schalleri)

Day's spike-tailed paradise fish (Pseudosphromenus dayi)

impressive emperor cichlid (*Aulonocara nyassae*), also from Lake Malawi, and the splendid fairy cichlid (*Aulonocara jacobfreibergi*).

Species endemic to Lake Tanganyika are the members of the genre *Neolamprologus* (which almost all used to be classified under the genus *Lamprologus*). This group counts almost 35 species, many of which are kept and bred in aquariums. They include the delicate lyretail cichlid (*Neolamprologus brichardi*) and several species known as shell dwellers (*Neolamprologus* sp.) because they need empty snail shells in which to lay their eggs. After the young hatch, they stay in the safety of the shell for some time, returning there whenever danger lurks.

The Lake Malawi cichlids are all mouthbrooders, which means the eggs incubate in the mouth of the female (or more rarely the male). The young also spend their first two or three days there, safe from harm. The Lake Tanganyika cichlids, on the other hand, are either cave or mouthbrooders. Lake Tanganyika is some six million years old, compared to Lake Malawi's mere million. This is why more behaviours and specialised species have developed in the former. Nevertheless, all the cichlids kept in our aquariums are interesting and worthwhile pets, which can be recommended primarily for the advanced beginner.

admirers who spread it throughout Europe during the following 25 years. It originally comes from Thailand and Cambodia and has been bred in many colour mutations over the decades. Males and females differ in colour intensity as well as fin size: the males are more colourful and have substantially larger fins. Some breeds are known as veiltailed fighting fish for their long, flowing fins and tail. Full-grown, they are about 6–7 cm in length, with brilliant red, greed, dark brown or blue colouring. The males cannot be kept

*Male Siamese fighting fishes (*Betta splendens*) sparring*

Fighting fish, ready for a fight

Paradise fish pair (Macropodus opercularis) *courting*

together in the same tank because, as their name indicates, they will end up fighting—biting each other's fins and in some cases even killing each other. However, a single male can be kept together with two to four females in a single-species or community tank. Of all the fighting fish species, Betta splendens is the easiest to keep. The minimum size of tank for a pair should be at least 50 litres, with a water temperature of about 25–26 °C. You needn't concern yourself here with pH value and total hardness.

Siamese fighting fish prefer live or frozen food, or will eat a flake food that contains both animal and vegetable ingredients.

The paradise fish
(Macropodus opercularis)

The paradise fish is the ideal beginner's fish, with which it is hardly possible to go wrong! It tolerates any water hardness found in our tap water and any pH value. In its native East Asia it often lives in flooded rice fields, pools and flat ponds, in which it can easily find a hiding place. The paradise fish can grow up to 10–11 cm long, but in the aquarium rarely grows longer than 6–8 cm. The males are among the most beautiful of the ornamental fishes, with the females close behind. As with other bettas, the paradise fish males do not get along well and tend to fight fiercely. The fish should therefore be kept in pairs, in tanks no smaller than 70 litres. It is advisable not to line the back and sides of the tank with any of the more delicate plants, such as milfoil, but instead to choose more robust greenery, such as long-leaved *Echinodorus* and *Cryptocoryne*, or *Vallisneria*.

One very important thing to remember is that the tank must be kept covered: paradise fish like to jump and if the tank is left open, you will soon have lost one.

Kissing gourami
(Helostoma temmincki)

Paradise fish pair, spawning

Courting pearl gouramis
*(*Trichogaster leeri*)*

Blue or marbled gourami
*(*Trichogaster trichopterus*)*

and swaying. They will lay anything from 200 up to 500 eggs, from which the fry will hatch in about one and a half days. The young will remain in the nest for about four days and then go off on their own. Feeding them presents no problems. You can alternate between live and dried food, which should be appropriate to their small size.

Somewhat larger than the paradise fish is the combtail (*Belontia signata*), up to 13 cm long. It should be kept only with other similarly robust fish, but is undemanding like the paradise fish.

In the following section we will briefly describe the three most popular gouramis. All are low-maintenance, although the dwarf gourami is somewhat fussier about water quality than the others.

The pearl gourami
(Trichogaster leeri)

The adults reach a length of 6, 10 or 12 cm. They come from southern and south eastern Asia, where they prefer standing and slow-flowing waters, including rice fields. They like somewhat dense vegetation—at the sides and back of the aquarium—but still need plenty of swimming space, through which they proceed placidly and without haste, or linger in one place for quite some time. Preferred water temperature is between about 22 °C and 28 °C, and closer to the upper limit of this range for mating.

The dwarf gourami (*Colisa lalia*) should not be kept together with larger species, and it also prefers to have its water changed at least partially in short intervals (20–30 % of the water weekly). The blue gourami, also known as the opaline or three-spot gourami (*Trichogaster trichopterus*)—of which there are various mutations such as the marbled and albino gouramis—and the pearl gourami are quite low-maintenance. Any pH and hardness value will do, and if the temperature drops to 20 °C on the odd occasion, this will not harm the fish at

If you wish to try breeding them, you will need a few floating plants, because the male arranges his foam nest right under the water's surface. For spawning, the pair must be put into a separate tank; otherwise, they would be disturbed by the other fish and would chase these away ruthlessly. If you raise the temperature a few degrees higher than 24–25 °C, the fish usually come quickly into mating condition. To make sure the fragile foam nest is not destroyed, you should switch off the filter and air pump—paradise fish are used to living in murky and oxygen-poor water. Their courtship ritual is wonderful to watch, a water ballet full of graceful movements

all; it should not happen too often, however, since they could eventually become sick over time.

Gouramis are omnivores, and the larger species in particular will eat anything that comes within their reach: live food, dry food, flakes, vegetables, pellets and tablets. We recommend a single-species tank containing ten to 12 fish. This will give you greater opportunity to observe their behaviour than you would have with a community tank.

Also included in the betta group are gouramis such as the dwarf croaking gourami (*Trichopsis pumilia*), the chocolate gourami (*Sphaerichthys osphromenoides*) and the honey gourami (*Colisa sota*). However, the last two of these are not suitable for beginners and should only be kept in an aquarium if you are able to offer them the specific biotope they need.

Bettas are excellent jumpers, so a good aquarium cover is an absolute must.

Dwarf gouramis
(Colisa lalia)

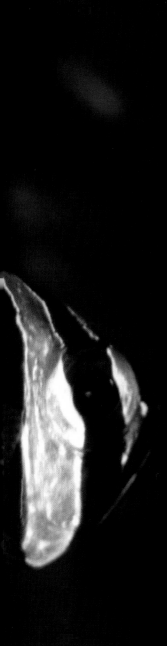

Public Aquariums

The first zoo in Britain was established in 1828 in London, and in 1853 the first aquarium followed, at Regent's Park in London. The early aquariums did not meet with much success because their fish did not survive long. The situation improved as awareness of habitat requirements increased and aquarists learned to aerate and filter the water. Over the last several decades, technological advances in water conditioning, aeration, heating and filtration, as well as the implementation of species-appropriate lighting have resulted in major improvements in aquarium habitats.

Behind all the exquisite display tanks is a lot of technology that the visitors never see, though it is essential for accommodating aquatic creatures from the world's tropical waters and sustaining them as long and as naturally as possible.

Aquarium display at the Institute for Marine Studies in Kiel, Germany

Many museums have wings or even separate buildings devoted to aquatic life. These are a great delight and resource for the fish-keeping enthusiast. Here one can draw insight and motivation from a variety of tank configurations and aquatic habitats, speak with the people who take care of the fish, and get technical advice from the curators.

Below are listed a few of the best-known aquariums of Britain having significant freshwater fish displays. These are wonderful places to visit, especially during those dark winter months, when you can be transported to a faraway underwater world and explore its magnificent colours and secrets.

- **Aquarium of the Lakes**
  Lakeside, Newby Bridge, Cumbria
- **Blue Planet, Cheshire Oaks,**
  Ellesmere Port, Cheshire

Glass fish (Chanda ranga)

- **Bolton Museum**
  LeMans Crescent, Bolton
- **Bournemouth Oceanarium**
- **Bristol Zoo Gardens**
  Clifton, Bristol
- **Chester Zoo Aquarium**
- **Deep Sea World**
  Battery Quarry, North Queensferry
  Fife, Scotland
- **Horniman Museum**
  100 London Road

  Forest Hill, South London
- **London Aquarium**
  Westminster Bridge Road, London
- **London Zoo Aquarium**
  Regent's Park, London
- **National Sea Life Centres at seven**
  locations throughout the UK including
  Birmingham, Blackpool, Scarborough
  and Weymouth
- **Stapeley Water Gardens**
  Stapeley, Nantwich, Cheshire

Index

Picture Credits

Angermeyer, Reinhard
    pp. 29, 31, 38 b., 40 t.,
    42/43 b., 92 b., 95,
    125 t., 162 b., 169 t., 171
Dennerle, Ludwig
    pp. 28 t. l., 56 b., 73 b.
Greger, Bernd pp. 58 t.,
    59 b., 62, 82 b., 141
Hagen p. 27
Kahl, Wally and Burkard
    pp. 6, 17, 19 t., 33 t.,
    40 t., 43 b. c., 50 t. and
    b., 51 b. l. and t. r.,
    52 t. and b. l. and r.,
    53 b. l., 54 t. and b.,
    55 t. and b. r., 58 b.,
    59 t., 64 t., 69 b.,
    72 t. and b., 78 b.,
    83 t., 85 t., 88 t., 89,
    101, 102, 103 t. and b.,
    104 b., 105 b., 109,
    110 t. and b., 111 t., 112,
    113 b., 116 l., 117 t. r.,
    121 t., 122 t. and b.,
    123 t. and b., 124 t.,

125 b., 128, 129 t.,
    130 b., 133 b., 137, 140,
    142 t. and b., 143, 144
    t., 145 t. and b., 146,
    147, 148 t. and b., 149 t.
    and b., 150 t. and c. l.,
    150/151 b. c., 151 t. r.,
    153 t., c. and b., 155,
    157, 158, 159 t. and b.,
    161, 163 b., 166, 170,
    172, 173, 177 t., 178 t.,
    179, 180/181, 184 b., 185
Paysan, Klaus pp. 55 b. l.,
    56 t., 70 b., 73 t., 97 t.,
    136, 167 t.
Redeleit, Wolfgang p. 83 b.
Reinhard pp. 121 b., 131 b.,
    132
Richter, Hans Joachim
    pp. 63 t. and c. r., 64 b.,
    65, 84, 90 t. and b., 91,
    92 t., 93, 94 t. and b.,
    96 t. and b., 97 b., 98,
    99 t., c. and b., 100,
    104 t., 105 t., 106, 107

t. and b., 108 t. and b.,
    111 b., 113 t., 124 b.,
    134 t. and b., 135 t. and
    b., 144 b., 151 b. r., 152,
    154 b., 156, 162 t.,
    164, 165, 174, 175, 176,
    177 b., 178 b., 182,
    183 t. and b., 184 t., 189
Silvestris pp. 8/9, 14/15,
    22/23, 34/35, 46/47,
    51 2nd and 3rd from t. r.,
    53 t. and b. r., 57 b. r.,
    60/61, 67 t., c. and b. l.,
    68 t. l. and r., 71, 74/75,
    77, 79 t. and b., 80/81,
    82 t., 85 b. r. and l.,
    86/87, 88 b., 114/115,
    117 b., 118/119, 126,
    129 b., 131 t., 138/139,
    186/187, 188
sera p. 76 b. r.
UMS p. 28 t. r.
Tetra p. 78 t.
All other pictures:
    Willi Dolder